Cracking
THE
Hard Class

Strategies for Managing the Harder than Average Class

Bill Rogers

Strategies for Managing the Harder than Average Class

Cracking THE Hard Class

Bill Rogers

P·C·P
Paul Chapman
Publishing Ltd

Text copyright © 1997 Bill Rogers
Illustrations copyright © 1997 Scholastic Australia Pty Limited

First published in Australia 1995 by Scholastic Australia Pty Limited

This edition first published 2000 by Paul Chapman Publishing Ltd.
Reprinted 2001

Paul Chapman Publishing Ltd
A SAGE Publications Company
6 Bonhill Street
London EC2A 4PU

SAGE Publications Inc
2455 Teller Road
Thousand Oaks, California 91320

SAGE Publications India Pvt Ltd
32, M-Block Market
Greater Kailash – I
New Delhi 110 048

British Library Cataloguing in Publication data
A catalogue record for this book is available from the British Library

ISBN 0-7619-6928-4

Library of Congress catalog card number available

Printed in Great Britain by The Alden Group, Oxford

Contents

Acknowledgments   **7**

Explanation of acronyms used throughout this book   **8**

Introduction   **9**

Chapter 1
What makes a class 'hard'?   **14**

    What is a hard class?   14
    Put them all in one class?   18
    Labelling the class   19
    Shouting a class down (or up)   20
    Classes that aren't listening   21
    Short-term colleague support
      (safety valve)   22
    Making changes   23
      A healthy whinge   23
      Action planning   24
      Tracking students across classes   26
      Changing the seating plan   27

Chapter 2
Classroom meetings   **29**

    Holding a classroom meeting   29
    Open meetings   33
    Closed meetings   34
    Mini-class meetings   36
    Meetings to deal with put-downs   37
      Put-downs and teasing in class   37
      A class meeting to deal with negative
        language and put-downs   38
      Class meeting and group establishment   39

Chapter 3
Developing a group (class) behaviour plan   **41**

    Basic steps in developing the
      behaviour plan as a 'class contract'   43
      Rights   43
      Basic responsibilities   43
      Class rules   44
      Consequences   46

      Support for behaviour change   48
    The consequential chain   49
    Developing class rules by discussion   49

Chapter 4
Developing a class behaviour plan using group reinforcement   **52**

    Introduction   52
    The process   53
      Preparation   53
      Formation of groups   55
      The 'reward' system   56
      The process in operation   56
    Behaviour modification at lower
      primary level   57
    Maintaining the program   58
    Support from colleagues   59
    Students in co-operative working teams   59

Chapter 5
Establishing a class   **61**

    Lining up and entry to class   62
    Positional placing   63
    Clarifying cues for questions, discussion,
      attention and help   65
      Tactical pausing   65
      Cues for on-task attention   66
      The teacher-help board   66
    Planning for transitions   67
      Students without equipment   67
      Helpful hints   67
    Gaining attention   68
    Monitoring 'working noise'   69
    Dealing with disruptive behaviour   71
      In the up-front instructional phase of
        the lesson   71
      Corrective language   72
      In the on-task phase of the lesson   74
    Closing the lesson   76
    Encouraging the individual and the class   78
    Motivation   81
    Classroom management   82

Chapter 6
Following up with disruptive students 84

Guidelines for follow-up	85
Mirroring behaviour	88
The 4W Form	89
Managing a crisis situation: Time-out	90
Time-out practices	90
Staff survey: Exit/Time-out policy review	94
Classroom rotation	94
Follow-up and three-way facilitation	95
Students who refuse to stay back after class	96
Apologies	96
Detentions	97
Suspension and expulsion	99

Chapter 7
Patterns of behaviour and changing behaviour 100

First principles of behaviour management	100
Case study	102
Developing an individual behaviour management plan with behaviourally disordered students	104
Behaviour profile	104
Contract supervision and case-management	105
Context for behaviour planning	107
Sessions covering behaviour skills	109
Evaluating the program—a case study	112
Subsequent sessions	114
Goal disclosure	115
Goal-directed behaviours	115
Disclosing the goal	115
Key questions	116
Completing the goal disclosure	117
Behaviours associated with attention deficit disorder	119

Chapter 8
Relief teachers and the hard class 122

Challenges facing relief teachers	122
Supporting relief teachers	124
A brief word to relief teachers	125
When your class has given a relief teacher a hard time	128
Thoughts of three relief teachers	128

Chapter 9
Supporting colleagues 131

Supporting colleagues who struggle with a hard class	133
Developing skills of confidence	135
Mentoring	136
Key skill areas	137
Teacher beliefs and attitudes	140
Changing behaviour	143
Teacher bullying (students who bully teachers)	146
Case study	146
Individual and group bullying	147
Dealing with the bullying of teachers	148
Occupational stress	153

Chapter 10
Conclusion 155

Appendixes

1 Colleague Support— Staff Questionnaire	159
2 The 4W Form	162
3 Stop/Start behaviour plan	163
4 The 3W Sheet	164
5 No put-down zone	165

Bibliography 166

Acknowledgments

Many thanks, appreciation and admiration to the many colleagues who have allowed me to take demonstration lessons in difficult and challenging classes from Year 1 to Year 10, and a few in Year 11 as well. They didn't need much prompting. (I especially recall many difficult Year 8 and Year 9 classes in the past few years.) This book is as much your story as mine. We learned together in our ongoing teaching journey that a key factor in dealing with hard classes is the support of colleagues. I have seen teachers admit in front of their peers (sometimes with tears) how difficult and demanding *that* Year 1 or Year 8 class really is, and then show genuine and appropriate relief when other colleagues recount their struggles with that class or those students. This is the beginning of 'cracking the hard class'. The support of colleagues is the underlying theme of this book. My special thanks go to David, Robin, Greg, Debbie, Ros, Peter, Joy, Colleen, Don, Roxanne, Jo, Jackie and Rachel. Thank you for letting me share your experience with hard classes in this book.

My thanks to Linda Moorhouse, the ever-patient and efficient transmitter of scribbled biro into readable print. Scholastic has been continually supportive of this project—remember Shane, this was your idea. My thanks to Shane Armstrong and his team, and to Valerie Marlborough, the editor.

And, of course, thanks to my family: Lora, Elizabeth and Sarah. Their understanding and patience enabled me to get the project in on time.

Bill Rogers

Bill Rogers,
Melbourne, March 1997

EXPLANATION OF ACRONYMS USED THROUGHOUT THIS BOOK

ADD   Attention Deficit Disorder

ADHD   Attention Deficit Hyperactive Disorder

BD   Behaviourally Disordered

BDN   Bad Day Not Withstanding

BDS   Bad Day Syndrome

BEO   Behaviour Enhancement Outcomes

CS   Contract Supervisor

IBMP   Individual Behaviour Management Plan

LOTE   Languages Other Than English

ROR   Respect Others' Rights

STBS   Surfing the Brain Space

THB   Teacher Help Board

YOYOB   You Own Your Own Behaviour

Introduction

*He supposed that for a crowd of boys aged from eight to eighteen, for
the moment not under the direct eye of authority, they looked docile
enough, even perhaps verging on the well-behaved? In this and in
other ways they were quite unlike the boys in his favourite kind of
school story. These fictional boys either behaved like men of forty or
carried on like comic lunatics or were wasters, scapegraces, bounders.*

Kingsley Amis (1996), You Can't Do Both

Halfway through the year Tim was appointed as a maths/science teacher to
the local high school. As a teacher new to the profession he was pleased he
had a job, even if he was only covering a teacher who had gone on leave
(little did he know she had gone off on stress leave).

Tim's timetable loading included several periods with a really challenging
Year 8. It was clear within a week that he was really losing any sense of
control or direction with the group. There was constant calling out, butting
in, aimless wandering, lateness to class, task refusal and boys in ritualistic silly
play fights. As part of my consultancy I was asked to 'work with him' (three
weeks down the track).

I thought I would visit a couple of science sessions—informally—and then
set up some team teaching and mentoring. As I walked down the corridor I
could hear the loud multitudinous voices of a class 'over the top'. I could
also hear the teacher's high-pitched yelling—his voice getting higher with a
mix of pleading and urgency. It sounded (as it was) chaotic. I walked in—a
knock on the door wouldn't have been heard.

I saw, in an all-encompassing scan of the room, a student pushing another
out of the window or at least it looked like that. I knew the boy who was
doing the 'pushing' (thank goodness it was the ground floor); or was Robyn
clutching him and coming back into the classroom via the window? Who
knows? It was entertainment for the audience of their peers: a male and
female student wrestling 'through' a window!

Justin, an ectomorph with ripped jeans, huge gym shoes and a blatant rock
T-shirt, was grappling with what looked like Robyn's diary.

9

Tim looked totally fazed. He gave me a look that said 'Help!' and 'I'm out of it'. I raised my voice: 'Justin, Justin!' The class looked around, unsure of what I would do. Justin turned. I repeated, 'Justin!' Lowering my voice, I directed Justin to leave the room. I turned to Robyn, 'Robyn—back to your table now. Justin, outside now! Now!' There is no guarantee when one gives unilateral commands. They are high risk and bluff—I don't use them often. Justin threw Robyn's diary on the floor, marched across the room, head-butted the light switch and followed me down the corridor, muttering and swearing as I 'led' him to the administration area.

I found out later, on the internal grapevine, that Tim's timetable slots with 8C had been given purposefully. 'Oh well, he was there to cover the other teacher—and, well, he was the last teacher in the allocation.' I argued that Tim was a first-year teacher and new to that school. 'Yes, but we all had hard times when we were at our first schools.'

Tim had received no emotional support—he'd been given the timetable, the curriculum materials and left to cope. Most of all there had been no preparation for the class, no structural or problem-solving support, and no clear direction about use of time-out or follow-up discipline strategies. At the staff meeting at the close of the day he stood up, fighting tears, explaining how he felt several weeks into the school year.

We then, *then*, tried to salvage his teaching career by setting up a considered support process. This process should have been set up from day one.

Credibility by 'proxy'

Credibility is an important factor with a difficult class. Credibility is earned over time through effective teaching, management skill and, most of all, fundamental respect that can keep the punitive side of management balanced with a commitment to dignity, welfare and solid encouragement (p 79).

In contrast to Tim's story, Maria (who had also 'picked up' another teacher's timetable) had come to a new school as a first-year teacher in Term 4. It was her first, significant, teaching load and she was understandably nervous. Fortunately the school had a strong commitment to supporting colleagues, especially in the area of teacher welfare and classroom management.

It was agreed that two classes in particular could well prove difficult for a newcomer to the school—especially a first-year teacher. The staff took a preventative approach and planned the first few lessons, within the unit of work, as a team. They also discussed discipline and referral approaches for after-class follow-up.

They strongly suspected, though, that if the teacher walked in on day one on her own, as it were, the students would give her a hard time. It was agreed that for the first few lessons the new teacher could establish herself 'by proxy' through team teaching. A senior colleague in the team who knew the students well would introduce Maria and then hand over the class but stay in the class for the first session.

Maria and the senior colleague discussed how the brief introduction would work, what Maria would say to introduce herself and what routines or rules she would refer to in Session One. The work for each session for each class was planned with her colleague. They wanted it to look, and sound, relaxed and natural—not as if she was the weak, new teacher who had to have an older, experienced teacher to keep control. They even discussed such issues as how to 'present' themselves to the class, where to stand, and the non-verbal aspects of presentation of oneself to a group.

The senior colleague 'settled' the class in the corridor and directed them into the room. As he stood front centre, Maria stood to one side, observing him and not looking at the class. He said, 'Good morning everyone. As you know, your regular teacher is on leave and Ms D will be your new teacher for Term 4.' At no point did he say Maria was a beginning teacher, or that 'I'm here to see you don't cause trouble!' (and so on).

On a pre-arranged cue he stepped aside and Maria went to the front (positional place—p 63) of the room and introduced herself, 'Good morning I'm Ms D. I'll be taking you this term for . . . ' She never mentioned she was a first-year teacher but added, 'I've taught in many schools [perfectly true] and it's a pleasure to be here.' She referred briefly to the relevant rules for her subject area and asked a student to put up a poster with several, positive headings on communication, respect, movement and learning (p 44). All the time she spoke, her senior colleague stood to one side as if to say 'I'm here to listen to Ms D, not watch you. I'm here to be part of (not control) your teacher's introduction to this class.' Had he stood watching, facing them, like a duty police officer, or like someone portraying the message that I'm the 'white knight' and nothing can go wrong while I'm here, his presence would have conveyed a different meaning. Maria and her colleague had discussed how to use confident, assertive correction for calling out, physical restlessness or lateness.

During the on-task phase of the lesson both teachers used correction and encouragement. Maria made a mental note of how relaxed and confident her colleague's language and style were. At the close of the lesson they resumed their 'positional places' at the front of the room. Maria reminded the students about homework and a smaller reminder slip was handed out. She went through the lesson closure and reminders about leaving the room tidy, and then stood at the door and said goodbye to the students individually as they left.

Maria felt positive about the session. The students were a lively group but she felt they had conveyed status on her 'by proxy'—they had accepted her as if through her colleague's role present in the room. Also, because she felt better, her teaching and management had been more effective.

They sat down later to plan the next lessons. They agreed that it might be beneficial if the senior colleague came in after the lesson establishment (during the on-task phase of the lesson) *au naturel*, as if to have a brief chat and then depart several minutes later. The school has an open-door policy, making such visits so much easier.

This approach has a number of benefits:
- The teacher has a positive start with a new class.
- There is two-way professionalism in planning and feedback with a special emphasis on establishment skills (p 61).
- Even apparently small issues such as the actual introduction, how colleagues deal with the introductory phase of the lesson, and cues for teaming have to be thought through.
- The class accepts the *new* teacher more readily within this approach.
- Most of all, the new teacher has a supportive entry into a hard-class setting and this support will extend to problem solving, lesson planning and discipline matters.

I have worked with scores of hard and difficult-to-manage classes at both primary and secondary levels. I have worked with teachers in these classes to re-establish a more positive working environment. We have worked together—sometimes with just the one teacher struggling, but often with the whole team at a particular year level. Often it has meant re-establishing the class (p 41), as well as working on behaviour management skills (p 71), following up with challenging students (p 84), improving confidence levels (p 135), and developing personal behaviour plans with behaviourally disordered individuals (p 104).

RIGHT... you pack of animals you! I can hear you down the back. Who do you think you are, eh?!!

Whatever we've done, though, we've emphasised an approach involving the support of colleagues. We've worked as a team avoiding the easy blame of:
- 'Yes, well, what do you expect with a group like 8D. They're all animals.'
- 'You'll never get anywhere with this class!'
- 'Anyway, he's a weak teacher. What do you expect— no wonder the class is a riot!'

Blaming the teacher or students is naturally tempting. However, as a long-term solution, it isn't a solution—it's a reaction. Natural maybe, but not helpful.

Reading the riot act may temporarily assuage things but it does little for the feelings or professional esteem of the teacher(s) in that class. A class that already has a reputation is not going to change on the strength of a five-minute lecture.

There is not one simple, single strategy that can change a hard class, just as there is no single reason for a class to be (or become) so idiosyncratically difficult. What my colleagues and I have found is that we have been much more effective when we have addressed the hard-class issue *whole school* (from a year level and team basis). That is the central, underlying theme of this book— we need the support of our peers to 'crack' the hard-class syndrome.

All examples and accounts used in this book come from our collaborative journeys. Where appropriate and necessary, I have modified some accounts and changed the names of students and teachers to protect the self-esteem of all, while keeping to the central integrity of the event or situation.

It is my hope that this book will help in addressing a challenge faced by many teachers today—why is this particular class *so* difficult? What can we do together to change things? How can we get out of the spiral of defeat and low expectation to enhance success in learning and social interaction? Most of all, how can we support one another?

Bad day notwithstanding

There are many strategies, approaches, skills and ideas outlined in this book. Within the safety of print, however honestly issues are faced, it all *sounds* probable, possible and even achievable. And so it is—bad day notwithstanding (BDN).

I have had many, many hard classes in my years as a teacher, and I have had to cope with some very challenging and disturbing individuals. When you think of it, every intransigent and disturbed adult, every petty thief, every hardened criminal and every twisted deviant human was once in someone's classroom (unless they had home education). In their embryonic forming that hard reality is the challenge of most teachers. We can't predict, although we're tempted, who such future persons will be (thank goodness). John Embling (author of *Fragmented Lives*, 1987) reminds us through his work with disturbed, dysfunctional children that we should not condemn the 'lost' to the 'kingdom of nothingness'. He states that schools can provide 'badly distressed *children* (author's italics) with a safe environment for learning, for interacting with others, for finding some pastoral relief to the nightmare of their lives. This means caring, humane environments, not jungles of violence and mayhem' (the *Age*, 2 June 1987, p 22). Yes, I have seen schools work successfully with difficult students and difficult classes. Such success, though, is hard won. And no matter how caring, how skilful, how well organised, how thoughtful the curriculum, how positive the language and how supportive our colleagues, there is the bad-day syndrome (BDS).

We'll shout on some days, we'll lose (actually *find*) our temper, and we'll say the wrong or inappropriate thing. Tiredness, frustration, irritation and social injustice will strike us, plus feelings of being fed up with the unsupportive bureaucracy and the mounting pile of marking. We will be having a bad day—something that should be eminently forgivable (in self and in others). A teacher in one of my seminars once said, 'I don't have bad days! I have bad weeks!' Fair enough.

We can cope with BDS, as can our students, if we're adult enough to acknowledge, apologise (where necessary), learn from it and move on. As Noel Coward once said, 'The secret of success is the ability to survive failure.' The issue of failure, stress and change is explored later in Chapter 9. My point here is that, in a *naturally* stressful job such as teaching, BDN should be a normative caveat to anything I've written.

Chapter 1

WHAT MAKES A CLASS 'HARD'?

What does make a class 'hard'? A bad year? Possibly. A reputation class (5A, 8D, 10L)—no doubt; a class that seems to have an *esprit de corps* expressed in group noise, resistance to normal classroom management and learning.

- 'It seems like a whole lot of brushfires around your room; you settle one thing down and something else starts!'
- 'It's the noise level—when I walk in it's like being in the playground.'
- 'I come out of 8D exhausted . . . thank goodness I've only got them for four periods!'
- 'It's like they hijack every lesson; hardly anything gets done!'
- 'It's not one or two students . . . Lee calls out, Kevin shouts back; Lisa and Cassie are chatting away privately while I'm trying to teach. In wanders Ahmed and Nazim late—that's not too bad but all their mates start up: "Whoa, late, eh? Naughty!" It's the seemingly constant hassle of trying to settle them down even before I can begin to teach.'

Hard classes are those whose allocation on the timetable is likely to induce a rapid headache.

Even experienced teachers find such classes a struggle. Most teachers have had at least one class like this in their teaching career. If you've taught next door to a hard class, their 'corporate' behaviour can have a through-the-wall effect on your class. And, cruel fate, such classes are sometimes handed out (in the worst timetable slots) to new, even beginning, teachers—so much for teacher welfare.

Cracking a hard class isn't easy once it has a reputation. Of course, early intervention is not only desirable but also essential. However, many teachers want to feel that they can deal with such classes by themselves—to admit struggle or defeat early is seen as a sign of weakness in the profession. There's the anomaly and yet the earlier the signs of 'hard class' are seen and acknowledged, the easier it is to intervene and change things.

What is a hard class?

Classes can be considered 'hard' when the *frequency* and *intensity* of the disruptive behaviour of a number of its members are significantly affecting the welfare of one or more of their teachers. Such behaviour is also significantly affecting any sense of productive teaching and learning. The other factor is *duration*. If the behaviour of the class (not just one or two members) is well beyond the BDS, it needs to be addressed as a hard-class issue across the whole-year level.

One of the confounding factors here is that sometimes a class is hard selectively, for just one or two teachers. This may be due to curriculum delivery, teacher style, personality, management or discipline approaches. In these cases it is better to work with the individual teachers and the class rather than develop a year-level or whole-school plan. These teachers, though, will still need the support of colleagues to turn the class around.

All the approaches and skills discussed in this book will be relevant in any hard class.
- Sometimes it's as amazingly basic as the organisation and timetabling of the classes. Having a school policy of deliberately streaming classes (ability streaming) can often create groups of students who believe and act out their label—'the vegie class' or 'the stupid class'. There is often a correlation between deliberately skewed groups of *learning-problem students* and problems in behaviour. It may well be that the curriculum offered to such students is couched (unintentionally) around a deficiency model. Such classes miss the opportunity of learning from more able peers— indeed they often experience the opposite. (Jones and Tucker's practical book (1990) on mixed ability teaching.)
- Sometimes it's the actual physical areas where teacher and students have to work.
- Sometimes it may be associated with the grouping of students. Most schools work hard at their groupings year by year. If it is known, though, that certain students are catalysts for others' disruptive behaviour, a change will have to be made for everyone's benefit.
- Sometimes the hard class is known by all but is given to the teacher new to the school or even to the first-year teacher. Obviously, classes should be allocated with some consideration given to these new teachers.
- Sometimes it is the subject area and how it is taught. Some students are more disruptive in subject areas they believe are not beneficial to their perceived needs. I've been in classes where students have effectively said, 'Well, we stuff around and that 'cos we hate doing . . . [the subject area], and this way we don't have to do it, do we?' Teachers in other faculty areas—deemed to be of higher educational value or merit—may be covertly adding to the culture of selective subject resistance.
- Sometimes it is the beliefs of the teachers that affect their perception of the class and hence their behaviour outcomes with that class. A teacher may label a class as 'All animals—they *never* listen' or 'I can't get anywhere with them'. Such easy labelling may affect how that teacher feels about, and relates to, individuals in the class who may well be behaving positively. There is ample research to show that one's emotional state is not simply the result of external factors. People bring beliefs to events that can significantly affect emotion and behaviour. That is why teachers A, B and C can all have different outcomes with the same class. It is not just skill, experience, management and enthusiasm—the more demanding a person's beliefs about others, the more stressed they are when social reality seems to contradict such beliefs (Bernard 1990; Rogers 1992). A teacher who characteristically believes, and whose self-talk repeatedly attests, that children *must* behave respectfully and appropriately at all times will find it much harder to work with sulky

students easily predisposed to challenge teacher authority. Such teachers will interpret the sulky reply to a question or direction as a major assault on their authority. Non-verbal behaviours such as sighs, pouts, raised eyebrows, frowns, slowness and clicking of tongues take on a significant malignant hue instead of being seen as 'normative' student behaviour. This is not to argue that we ignore such behaviour, but it is important to put such behaviours into perspective. A teacher may say, 'Well, I like respect and I want respect, but it takes time to get it with these kids. I'm not going to get stressed out on this. Some students will like me and respect me, some won't—it's self-defeating and anti-reality to demand otherwise.' This kind of cognitive reframing is healthier and enables one to feel better. When we feel better we do better. We need to back up any rational self-talk with thoughtful and effective teaching management.

- Sometimes colleagues are not given the opportunity to explore the hard-class problems and look at whole-school solutions (or at least year-level solutions). In other words, there is a lack of colleague support if the hard class is not addressed on this basis.

- Sometimes it is the closed-door syndrome—literally. In the past some teachers, including me, saw their classrooms as their physical, educational and managerial domain. This is understandable. But other teachers go beyond this to a psychological closed-door mentality. I have seen colleagues plaster the inside of their windows (on both passage and outside windows) with posters so that no one can see in. I have even seen a colleague totally block off the small glass section of his door. Is this privacy or anxiety about what passing observers might see? Many schools now have an open-door policy. The door is left half-open (purposefully) so a colleague can walk in, having knocked on the door first of course. It is important that even senior staff perform this little courtesy of knock, wait and then enter. I have often seen people abuse their rank by just barging in and taking over a class with no regard as to how a teacher might feel, and I'm not talking here about crisis situations either (p 22).

- Sometimes a class will sabotage a teacher's every attempt to manage the group. Most often this 'sabotage' is exercised by a few key, influential students who garner active (or passive) acquiescence in their peers.

- Students sometimes pick their teachers as targets; they weigh up very early that this teacher is 'weak' in their eyes. They pick up on tone, manner, body language and the interactive responses and conclude that they can have fun with this teacher. Some students will crow and gloat over how they sent teacher X 'packing', or reduced them to tears, or to a rage. Some students will even bully teachers to satisfy their own pathetic sense of power and control (p 146).

- Conversely a class sometimes goes wrong because of the way it is treated. There are teachers who believe they can control by fear, intimidation or frequent criticism. They use unnecessarily punitive measures, group detentions and mean-spirited discipline. They are not averse to intentional embarrassment, sarcasm and public ridicule. Quite apart from the professional morality of such an approach, many students will not accept it. Students will find ways to pay back such a teacher. (I've even seen students go on strike.) Children today are keenly aware of their rights, especially the right to fair treatment, the right to have a say in how things are, and especially the right of reply when in disagreement with their teacher.

- Sometimes key powerbrokers in the class have been allowed to become catalysts for disruptive behaviour across the class. There are always several powerbrokers in a hard class; they've learned how to 'work the group' to satisfy their needs for power and attention. It is important not to let these students act as gladiators in a cheering bear pit. Excesses of freedom of one or two students have been confused with attitudinal mitigation of a student's circumstances (p 19). These students need an early message that they will be given plenty of support and understanding of 'where you're coming from', but that cannot be confused with 'allowing you to hijack teaching/learning and safety in our classrooms'. Persistent disruptors need to be given a clear choice to work with class (and personal) behaviour plans or be relocated to other classes. No one or two students have a right to hold a class 'to ransom', as it were. We need to cater for all the stakeholders. We can build up the silent majority, engaging their silent disapproval into active disapproval and refocused behaviour. Thoughtful use of classroom meetings (p 29), classroom contracts (p 41) and personal behaviour plans (p 104) can empower the silent majority and enlist their support. By making certain rights-infringing behaviour unpopular we can enlist the moral support of the group.

- A common reason for the hard-class issue is that some teachers have not established the class well. They have not discussed the rules and routines necessary to enable rights and responsibilities to be clarified. It is important to *teach* a class reasonable entry and exit routines, seat plans, rules for class discussion, simple cues for asking questions or getting teacher support, workable 'noise' levels, basic classroom agreements for learning and respectful treatment, and so on. There are many routines that need to be developed in the first few days and weeks with every class, but especially with the harder class. These are discussed in Chapter 5. Effective teachers will not allow (not establish) poor patterns of behaviour because they know that in doing so they establish a pattern that is hard to change further down the track. They use management skills and techniques that can balance corrective leadership with encouragement. These skills are transferable and can be developed through supportive peer mentoring. Most of all, such teachers follow up and follow through early with disruptive students, especially the ringleaders and powerbrokers. These teachers are not averse to colleague support in any form because they know that it is only by working with colleagues that problems can be shared, stress can be managed and solutions can be found—not perfect solutions but workable ones.

Put them all in one class?

Why not put all the difficult students in one class—a sort of 'hoon' class—as one brave principal suggested to me (an option he would never have been willing to entertain *personally*).

This novel approach sounds, on the face of it, eminently sensible for everybody (except the teacher who actually has to teach such a class). Putting all the difficult and reputation students into one class would result in the following:

- There would be almost no significant role modelling of reasonable social and on-task learning behaviour by students in the 'normal' behaviour range.
- Behaviour management is significantly more difficult as key power brokerage and hierarchical pegging take on a more challenging, even dangerous, shape than in a regular class.
- Such a class also gets its special reputation beyond any normative hard class that has a distribution of students with challenging behaviours.
- In one sense, too, it is unfair for the teacher and students—there is an isolated mentality for both.

I'm not saying such a project cannot work but to set it up within a school environment sends the message that we can't contain you—the troublemakers—within the relative normality of a classroom setting.

It will be more effective if the school can set up a *partial* withdrawal of difficult students to give educational and behavioural support one-to-one or in small groups (p 105). In such groups key learning and behaviour skills can be taught through dialogue, active teaching and role modelling. Furthermore, by regularly being in normative class settings they are subject to the social pressure of their peers. If their behaviour in these normative class settings is so disruptive that learning and safety rights are affected, then school-wide discipline, including loss of privileges through time-out and withdrawal from certain areas, will be involved. The message for behaviourally disruptive (and behaviourally disordered) students is the following:

- You are always welcome in our classes and our school but not with behaviours that continually and significantly affect the rights of others.
- Your behaviour is your 'choice' even though your behaviour is affected by conditions, backgrounds and experiences outside the school setting. Our message will be, however, that when you come into *our* school this is how *we* do things. We can help you to make better, more effective choices.
- 'You own your own behaviour (YOYOB). I don't own it, your mates don't own it, and your mum doesn't own it. You do.' This is the parallel to the 'choice' idea. This doesn't deny the need to help, support and encourage students with their behaviour. But it doesn't mean students are merely victims of their poor habituation or life's circumstances.

Labelling the class

Labels are useful in their way—a kind of summary. However, when it comes to global labels used within the context of a whole class they are perceptually hindering. Labels such as '*all* these kids are animals, idiots, dropkicks . . .', 'these kids *never* . . .' or 'these kids *always* . . .' are global in definition. Such global labelling significantly affects perceptions and beliefs about the whole class, let alone key powerbrokers, and may make it difficult for teachers to alter their judgment. Actions that are open to a wide range of interpretations tend to support prior labels and hence reinforce prior perceptions and beliefs.

Walking down the corridor to team teach with a colleague he remarked, 'Well, you're going to work with my animals today, are you?' That's how he saw them (no hint of humour in his voice). As soon as we were in the room a student called out some inane comment (I saw it as low-grade attention seeking). My colleague looked at him and said to me (loudly), 'I told you, didn't I, eh?' Actually, in the whole lesson only half a dozen boys and one girl were disruptive, and it was all low level—annoying but low level. My colleague saw, and blamed, the whole class for the behaviours of these students. We had (I believed) a reasonably successful science lesson together but my colleague couldn't see it that way.

One of the ways to change perceptions is to discuss the same class and key individuals with other colleagues. That may help. I've sat in case conferences where some colleagues cannot find any redeeming features in a student(s):
- 'How dare they . . . ' (they did.)
- 'I can't stand it when they act like idiots!'
- 'No way! Those students will not, I repeat not, behave that way.' (They did.)

I am not unsympathetic to these frustrations (I've felt like maiming a student from time to time, I've shouted and I've got angry), but I've put it down to fallibility—mine and theirs. Even when there is intentional fault and blame, harbouring long-term resentment is damaging (very damaging) to oneself and one's professional role. It's not worth it. We can deal with key individuals in the class with:
- thoughtful after-class chats (p 85)
- constructive conflict resolutions
- thoughtful use of classroom meetings (p 29)
- problem solving with the support of colleagues.

We can often turn around both individuals and the class, or at the very least we can make things better than they are.

Shouting a class down (or up)

You've heard it, done it or certainly felt like doing it: 'Shut up! Shut up or I'll . ! !' (I'll what?). I've heard colleagues from several classrooms away, shouting and even yelling. It's tempting. It sounds strong.

I'm not talking about raising our voice from time to time when it's appropriate. I'm talking about shouting a class down. It feels as though we're in control when we shout. It satisfies some teachers—it feels as though they've got back at the class. Worse, some teachers add to the shouting the unsolicited lecture: 'And where do you think you'll be, eh? eh? With that kind of behaviour, where will you end up, eh? Unemployed; that's where! When I was at school . . .'

If it works at all—and it might the first time—it has a limited life span. How do we top it? Do we keep shouting to settle them down *each lesson*? And what do they learn from our shouting? By shouting, or using a *frequently* loud voice, we are (in effect) training the students that this is the way it has to be. Furthermore, shouting or frequent and extended use of a loud voice, or snappy tone of voice, unsettles, unnerves, overly excites or even entertains the class.

Settling down a noisy class is never easy but shouting will not work in the long term—and loud teachers correlate with loud classes. It's worth discussing the class-settling options with colleagues in your team; or, better still, watch effective colleagues to see how their verbal and non-verbal behaviour is communicating calmness to the class.

Effective class-settling options are:

- waiting, standing relaxed and just waiting (silent, casual, look at the watch—not overdone though) and then use the choice of words that indicates what you expect to happen ('settle', 'face this way', 'listen' and 'By the time I've counted to 20 I want you all sitting on the mat')
- moving around for brief, 'private' chats and then moving to the positional place at the front of the room
- using a small handbell, clapping rhythm, silent teacher hand-up cue (as a private signal) or even (at secondary level) light tapping of a glass to indicate you expect a change in residual noise level—then a tactical pause so we can give our first verbal direction
- writing on the chalkboard while the residual noise drops (I sometimes draw a little cartoon and write 'settling down, thanks everyone') and then wait (tactical pause) and give the first group direction.

It is hard to have any effective teaching and learning if there is not a clear, calm, focused start for a class.

Classes that aren't listening

A few years ago in Belfast, I was asked to take a session on teacher stress (a high school staff meeting). Prior to the meeting the principal asked if I would take a couple of Year 7 classes (to 'get an impression'). We walked down a corridor—I could hear the class a mile away. The principal knocked on the door and a harried-looking colleague opened the door. Behind his head I saw several rows of grinning, noisy, unfocused students. The principal said, 'This is Mr Rogers from Australia. He'd like to take your class.' 'Good,' was the teacher's reply, and he then walked off with the principal down the corridor.

Rather than try to 'get' them quiet by standing at the front of the class and directing them, I walked to the chalkboard, rubbed clean a space and began to draw a map of Australia. I whistled a tune (conveying, I hoped, my confidence and calmness) as I drew sharks, a sun, and a touch of blue here and there. I then wrote on the chalkboard, 'I'm an Australian.' (I knew they'd probably all be watching the TV program 'Neighbours'. It's on twice a day in the UK). All the while they called out, 'Oi, who are you!?', 'What are you doing here?' and 'You deaf?'. But the overall noise level was dropping with each artistic addition to the chalkboard. I then wrote, 'When you've settled, folks, I'll explain. Ta.'

When the residual noise (helped by communal shushes and 'shut-ups') dropped enough I turned and stood, relaxed and still, waited and then started.

When I'd introduced myself (the teacher, you see, hadn't even introduced me) the first student question was, 'Hey, do you know what's right up to date about the "Neighbours" episodes?' I racked my brains; I'd hardly watched it. We had a useful cultural exchange. By staying calm myself and giving them a focus the students had settled. No guarantees, but it was better than just shouting.

I have also worked with a number of very challenging classes who, *en masse*, demonstrate an indifference to whoever walks in and stands up-front trying vainly to engage group attention and motivation. With one home group in an open-plan school, I could have stood at the front and raised my voice, and it might have worked. However, I decided to leave the positional place up-front and purposely wander the room. I decided to become 'known' by establishing myself *en route* around the room. I wandered and had a private chat with each mini-grouping. I walked over to the group at the back and said, 'Good morning, my name's Bill Rogers; I'll be taking you for English.' I held out my hand and asked for names. Most responded. I had unsettled them by roving into their 'territory' as they perceived it. Ten minutes later I went up to the front—the 'normal' teacher position (p 63). Having remembered some key names I called for group attention. I was banking on the fact that this mini-establishment (around the class group) would enable group establishment. 'OK everyone, settle down thanks. [Pause] I need you facing this way and listening. [Pause] Thanks Dean, [pause] Craig, [pause] Darren, [pause] Rebekkah, [pause] and Paul. [Pause] It is Paul isn't it?' He grinned back, 'Yeah, it's Paul!' They were 'settled' now (several leaning back, still suspicious, a lot of wry, grinning faces). I introduced myself formally, 'I've already met you, but I'd like to say good morning to you all and explain why I'm here today.'

Now, of course, these approaches imply a sense of personal confidence and self-esteem. I have learned not to be overconfident or believe that any one approach will always work. If the worst comes to the worst we have to use approaches such as crisis management and time-out (p 90).

I cannot really control others. I can only control myself (and that's a challenge, especially when tired, frustrated, overworked . . .).

Short-term colleague support (safety valve)

I have walked past many classrooms where marginal (even significant) chaos is in progress—much more than healthy working noise or appropriate fun.

In many schools I can't simply walk past such a class thinking, 'Well, I'm glad it's not me' or 'I'm glad I haven't get that lot!'. These schools have adopted (among many other supportive measures) a 'safety-valve' option that colleagues can feel free to use if they want to give *immediate* support to a colleague. Such support is as follows:
- Knock on the (riotous) door and inform your colleague there's a message for them at the office. This is code for 'take a break while your passing colleague takes your class'. There needs to be a no-blame climate for this to operate well.
- Ask the teacher if you could 'borrow' a couple (or several) students— name the catalysts —and then direct them to another class (for brief time-out) or have a chat with them out of sight of the room. No doubt the rest of the class will have some suspicions but there's enough ambiguity about the withdrawal to give the class teacher a chance to regroup. Most of all it is carried out without any imputation that our colleague is a 'weak teacher'.
- Send a student messenger to the class to the effect that Ms E wants to see these students (named) in Room 22.

It is important to knock on the colleague's door (it's good modelling) unless crisis management is required. These safety-valve options are merely temporary relief for our colleagues, like the red-card option for the exit of a very disruptive student (p 92). However, if these options are not backed up with significant problem solving, restructural support (p 41) and personal behaviour plans with behaviourally disordered students, they will be of little value.

Making changes

I had just taken a difficult Year 8 class as a 'demonstration class' for other teachers. During the lesson one of the students, Michael, had gone through several attention-seeking episodes (I should have sent him off to time-out, but no, stupidly, I battled on). He jumped up onto a table, and leaped higher still with his hands reaching for the open metal beam. He hung by his hands, emitting baboonish noises. Several of the boys cheered and laughed as I moved across to his hanging feet. I had no bananas and so I said, 'Michael, if you're not down by the time I count to ten, I'm going to climb up and seriously tickle you.' He dropped like a stone and said 'Sh_t! you're not touching me!', and raced off out of the classroom (self-imposed time-out). At least I was able to resume my activity with the class.

In the staff workshops I conducted at the end of the day the first question from the staff was, 'How did you manage with Michael and 8D?'. When I shared my struggle with the class and his baboon stunt the common response was wearied grins and 'good'. They weren't revelling in an outsider's failure or bad day. Rather they were, in effect, saying your struggle (as an outsider) legitimates our struggle. Students such as Michael are difficult to work with in a normal, typical, school setting. By having a healthy whinge about our struggles, our successes and the seemingly impossible tasks, we can get somewhere with hard classes.

Michael was eventually sent off to a 'special unit'. In the meantime we'd had him on an individual behaviour management plan, used in-school suspension and had withdrawn him from several classes for safety reasons. 8D dramatically improved.

We won't always be successful with students like Michael—this is reality. We have to have the options of suspension, even expulsion, and alternate 'education' settings to support schools. Weighing up the rights of everyone is never easy but it has to be just. Safety, fair treatment and fundamental learning can't be compromised because of a few students.

A healthy whinge

After the debacle with Michael's class we had a really healthy whinge! I got all the teachers together who taught 8D (and combinations of 8D) and we had a clearing of the air. This is important. While most teachers avoid labelling students and whole classes (p 19), it's natural to want to sound off about the episodic stress caused by students like Michael.

I have been in countless faculty and staff meetings (as well as ad hoc meetings) where we've 'let off steam'. We've released the tension of having to teach a group like 8D. The sharing of bad feelings is cathartic—up to a point. However, *just* whingeing or getting locked into self-defeating dialogue ('We can't get anywhere with them' and 'It'll never change') stifles problem solving.

Problem analysis has to follow a whinge with colleagues, and lead us to action planning involving colleague support. There's always something that can be done with a hard class. But if changes are going to occur they need some structure that arises from reflective and substantial colleague support.

Action planning

Initially, it may seem all too much: the way that class pushes and shoves in line, the noise levels, the silly calling out, the physical restlessness, the five-minute settling, the dealing with one incident after another, the off-task behaviour, the lack of work produced—where do we start?

It is essential that the hard-class phenomenon is addressed at the earliest intervention possible. Do not let it degenerate into a Term 2 or Term 3 problem where teachers' energy levels have been significantly sapped by the class and they have almost lost any goodwill necessary for making changes.

1 Firstly it needs to be ascertained whether it is a hard class for all the teachers at that year level or grade, or whether only one teacher (or a few) finds it difficult to manage the class. It doesn't take long to ascertain how wide the reputation of a class is at secondary level. If several teachers are struggling it will be necessary to call a special year-level meeting to address the issue, as early in Term 1 as is possible. If it is genuinely only one subject teacher struggling with 9E or 10B then it will be more effective to work just with that teacher and class using the several approaches outlined later:
   • a classroom meeting
   • a classroom contract where the class/subject teacher goes through a re-establishment phase
   • a group reinforcement activity
   • individual behaviour management plans for particular students.

2 A year-level meeting can acknowledge that several teachers are finding 7E or 8D a challenge. This is, in itself, useful. 'It's not my fault' is an often-heard expression at this meeting. After a normal whinge about the group the co-ordinator of the meeting will raise the *key questions* to ascertain the extent of the problem, how different teachers see the class and individual behaviour(s), and what they are currently doing to address the issue.
   • *How* 'hard' is this class? What do we mean by 'hard' (give specific examples)?
   • Is the class worse at any particular time of the week or day? It is

important that in answering this question colleagues are not smug about how well they manage 8D or 9C, even if they do not have the same degree of stress or hassle as others.

- Who are the ringleaders in the class? What behaviours do they typically engage in? With whom? With whom do they normally sit? Does it matter?
- Is the behaviour of the ringleaders different across subject areas? Do some students, for example, modify their behaviour from, say, maths to woodwork or is their behaviour consistently disruptive? How? If curriculum, lesson delivery and method are having an effect, what effect do we believe they are having? This is a difficult question because sometimes it is the curriculum material, its delivery and often a lack of commitment in catering for mixed ability that contributes to the hard-class aspect.
- Are any of us having *any* success with 6B, 8D or 9C? In what way?

3 Develop an action plan that is year-level based. Rather than having each teacher pursue their own plan, the team will do the following:
- Reassess how they have established their classes, and pursue the benefits of a common re-establishment across the year level through a classroom meeting (p 24) or whole-class contracts (p 41).
- Decide whether to go for some common rules and routines across 8D within a re-establishment activity, for example whether to have common working noise procedures, and entry and exit procedures, and whether to publish rules and expectations.
- Reassess short-term support if a class is in borderline chaos (p 22).
- Clarify the use of time-out for key ringleaders (students who act as catalysts for classroom disruption). Make sure the time-out plan is consistent in its application (p 90).
- Have an agreed procedure for 'tracking' behaviourally disordered students. If necessary, 'target' ringleaders for individual behaviour plans or if their behaviour is consistently and persistently disruptive, remove them from that year level and relocate the student in another year level with individual work programs. In a larger school it will be possible to relocate students across a year level. It can be helpful, firstly, to discuss with the student how their behaviour is significantly affecting learning (and safety in some cases) in that class and point out that they may have to face being relocated in another group. Make the choice clear, within a rights/responsibility focus. In some cases, the class may need to be split up—this is an exception and would occur only if the whole staff team believed that this would be the best option for the class group.
- Consider whether or not any colleagues have been subject to harassment or bullying. If this has been the case, set up due process *immediately* (p 150).

4 Decide on an action plan and the phases of implementation together. For example, the first step might be for all the teachers to run an open classroom meeting with 8D, then report back to their colleagues and develop their common action from those meetings. If the group is

significantly disruptive *en masse*, one meeting will be sufficient (p 34) to outline the concerns of staff to students and develop a classroom contract for use by all teachers who teach that particular group.

5   Implement and evaluate the plan over a term. There will need to be several meetings with colleagues down the track to finetune, share ups and downs, and plan for the following term. It can help to include the students in this evaluation.

Tracking students across classes

Students, even from reputation classes, do sometimes modify their behaviour in other classroom settings. It can be helpful then at both primary and secondary levels for teachers to 'track' students across classes other than their own. By observing students in other subjects/specialist areas we can get an understanding of how different teachers, settings and programs can affect group and individual behaviour. It is not a spy job—it is showing an interest in our students in other settings.

While I watched Karl in wood design making his CD stacker out of plywood, we chatted:
Student: 'Anyway, wotcha doing in here?' (in wood design)
Teacher: 'Oh, just wanted to see how 8D got on here, and see what sort of things you were making.'

I also spent time with Karl (and 8D) in textiles and was surprised at the gusto with which they addressed T-shirts and sewing machines. I noted with interest how the textiles teacher dealt with Karl's whingeing when the sewing machine wasn't free. She said, 'OK, what can you be doing while you wait for a free machine, Karl?' She refocused his responsibility within the task. It was also interesting to see how 'my' students responded with another teacher—the human dynamic in another setting.

As part of the team (the English faculty) I was trying to set up a year-level plan for 8D (p 41). I 'tracked' them across several subject areas beyond English. In graphic design Ben asked, 'Hey, you following us or what?' A big grin on his face indicated he'd 'sussed' me. He said, 'Look, you're not a normal teacher are you? I mean you're a shrink or something, eh? I've seen the way you work with us and the sort of stuff we do as a class. I've even seen you making some notes.' So I told him, 'Yes, I'm seeing how 8D operates across all subject areas. That's why you've seen me wandering in and out of your classes.' Here I mentioned how they had seen teachers from other classes when I'd been teaching 8D. The students will 'pick up' on what we're doing and it won't hurt to explain our purpose, but keep it low key. It is not helpful to over engage the curiosity questions. At the very least they'll know that all the Year 8 teachers are taking an interest in them.

When visiting another teacher's class it is helpful for the 'host' teacher to briefly introduce the 'visiting' teacher: 'Mr Rogers will be working with us later in the lesson. You know Mr Rogers from English.' At that point the visitor can move either to the far side up the front of the room (leaving the centre of the room for the 'instructing' teacher) or if there's a spare seat at the back the visitor can sit there (as unobtrusive as one can be). At that point the host teacher carries on with their 'normal' lesson or activity. The visiting and host teacher will have discussed the protocols of interclass visits and likely scenarios beforehand.

From such class-hopping, we can discuss the following:
- What are the main forms of disruptive behaviours? How is the calling-out, butting-in and task avoidance in this different setting? Does a change from, say, 'academic' subjects (so-called) to 'non-academic' subjects (for example, maths to woodwork) see any significant behaviour change? If so, what sort of changes? When visiting Karl in woodwork we talked about how he had drawn up the plan for his CD stacker in his workbook, and how he had demonstrated some thought and care in his writing. I commented on his effort and planning. He seemed pleased. This little journey of interest and encouragement seemed to have an effect back in the English classroom. Or at least it changed my perception of Karl (and maybe his perception of me).
- What are the power cliques like here? What seating plans occur in other settings? Does a seating plan help? Do we need to change the seating plan (see below). Do Nathan, Shane and Karl act as ringleaders or powerbrokers? Do such powerbroker positions change depending on subject area and setting? Teachers can use such analysis and feedback to further refine their group plan and also target individuals who may need special assistance or individual behaviour plans.

Changing the seating plan

Sometimes a change of seating may help, especially in a more 'formal' setting (English, history, maths and so on). Some teachers allow students to sit where they want; others use a draw-a-name-from-the-hat approach. But if students are given free rein: 'Sit where you want; we'll change it if it's not working', it is then harder to change the seating plans several weeks into the term. In one class I visited, almost the whole back row had formed a power clique. Tables set out in long continuous rows, for example, make it very hard for students to get in and out of their seating, causing several minutes of unnecessary mayhem at the outset of class time, as well as making it difficult for the teacher to move around the classroom.

One helpful approach we've used to correct an unhelpful seating organisation is to encourage the students to work with the teacher to rearrange seating options. We had a brief chat with the class about our concerns regarding seating and behaviour, and its effect on the whole class. We then handed out a sheet to everyone in the class with the following directions:

> As your teachers we are concerned about the level of noise during seat work. We are thinking about changing the seating plan and we need your help. Write down the names of two students you know you can sit with who won't hassle you (or vice versa) or make it difficult for you to get on with your classwork. We'll use your suggestions in the new seating plan.
>
> Thanks
> Mr Rogers

The students knew that we would use their suggestions but that the teacher was the final umpire. When the class came into the room the following week the new seating plan reflected their involvement. By engaging their support we had a better outcome for the teacher and learning in the subsequent weeks. That, coupled with a reconsideration of rule/routines/management practice and teaching methods, saw a much more relaxed and productive class (and teacher).

THE REPAIRER AND REBUILDER

There are teachers whose relational, managerial and collaborative skills single them out as key bridge builders. These are teachers who can go into hard-class settings, not as white knights, but as staff working with regular classes to repair and rebuild. Before the spiral of constant bad feelings, low expectations and burnout occurs, these colleagues can often set up classroom experiences that rekindle group spirit, re-establish a framework for educational and social harmony, and rework the delivery of curriculum to enable relative enjoyment and success. It can be helpful, especially at secondary level, for senior staff to be aware of where these talents are in their teams and utilise these skills as early as possible when a class, and its teacher, is losing the plot.

Roll over!

Chapter 2

CLASSROOM MEETINGS

*The task of the modern
educator is not to cut down
jungles but to irrigate deserts.*

C S Lewis

*I' the midst o' the body, idle and inactive,
Still cupboarding the viand, never bearing
Like labour with the rest; where the other instruments
Did see, and hear, devise, instruct, walk, feel,
And, mutually participate, did minister
Unto the appetite and affection common
Of the whole body.*

Shakespeare, Coriolanus, *Act 1, Scene 1*

When I read this dialogue, put in the mouths of Roman citizens by Shakespeare, my first thought was of a difficult Year 8 I'd worked with— a music class. 'I' the midst o' the body, idle and inactive . . . ' They were active, but the unhelpful kind! What we wanted to see from these Year 8 students was an 'appetite and affection common of the whole body . . .' How could we turn this class around?

These students had given their teacher 'hell', as she had described it. The music lessons had degenerated into teacher–student slanging matches, little on-task work and a feeling of constant frustration by the teacher whenever she faced the class. Several of the girls, in particular, were sullen, sulky and unco-operative. There was calling out, task avoidance, talking while the teacher was trying to teach and so on. Lessons were basically the 'horizontal tyranny' of the strongest class members.

Holding a classroom meeting

I encouraged my colleague to conduct a classroom meeting with the Year 8 students. My belief was that if we could invite their views, perceptions and feelings we could perhaps find some starting points for change. She had never run a classroom meeting and so we agreed to run it together, based on my observations of the class.

I joined my colleague for a lesson, just to observe what I've already noted above. In the last five minutes of the lesson I walked to the front and directed the attention of the students. They settled and I introduced myself and shared—briefly but specifically—what I'd observed in the past forty minutes. I said in a calm voice, conveying seriousness of tone as I scanned their now quiet faces, 'As a teacher in this school, I'm concerned, very concerned, about this class and how learning and behaviour are not going well. I'm *not* going to give you a lecture because you know better than anyone what it's like in music—here. I just want to invite you to have an open meeting with me and Mrs P next Tuesday to discuss what's really happening in music, why you think it's happening and how you believe we can change things here. We're going to have a classroom meeting. When you come in on Tuesday you'll see the chairs in a circle. I'll ask a student to keep a record of what we discuss and suggest together. I'll also ask a volunteer to write up our suggestions on the chalkboard.' Several hands went up, but the bell was about to go. I put up my hand to block questions and said, 'Look, I know you've got a lot of questions already, but think about it and be ready for next Tuesday.' I directed them to leave (p 76).

Already I felt that the teacher's current teaching style, discipline and curriculum delivery were key factors. Although she was an accomplished musician and a 'fine piano teacher' (in the words of a colleague), she had clearly lost most of this Year 8 class. And she agreed. As an older teacher she was very demanding on herself and at times intolerant of typical adolescent behaviours that could have been refocused with skill and a little enthusiasm. Some changes in teaching methods and some collaboration with the class would help. I thought about how I could assist her in these areas without discouraging her. That was difficult enough, but my real concern was what the students might say about her *as a teacher* at the classroom meeting. I discussed with my colleague how the students might react and what they might say when given a 'voice'. I didn't want her to be hurt. I wanted to work towards a co-operative model with teacher(s) and students.

The following Tuesday the students came in and name tags were given out to help me. They took their seats with some unease and laughter.

Once settled I explained what we would be doing for that class period.

Step 1   I said, 'I want firstly to hear what you have to say about how you feel things are in the class—both positive and negative views.' It is important as teachers that we show we do care for their input. When students are allowed to express their views freely it helps to clarify the problems, and why such problems exist in the perception of teacher and students alike. It also stimulates a more co-operative atmosphere that is united to problem solving. Most of all, it conveys genuine concern.

Some teachers are worried that the students will make ridiculous suggestions and some do. Some will make ambit claims. This too is normal. If the teacher manages this well within the rules, students soon bounce back to the more serious agenda. The main thing at this stage is to elicit their responses and not to put them down for their ideas or use the classroom meeting as a pulpit for our frustrations alone. It is important to use this first stage to reflect their point of view in order to clarify it, for example 'Are you saying . . .?' or 'You seem to be saying . . . Is that correct?' Reframing or paraphrasing their point of view without judging it is the hard part. Save any judgment until the end; the class can make its judgment within the fair test of how suggestions fit basic rights and responsibilities. When sharing your impressions and feelings it's important to remember some basic rules. Ask if anyone has any problems with the rules (p 31).

Step 2 'I'd like to share my concerns and feelings with you about how we see things here in music,' I said. Here we went through (briefly—no big added lecture) the behaviours, how we felt about them, and how we believed they had affected teaching and learning.

Students noted that a lot of lessons were boring because they do a lot of filling-in of sheets, theory and copying. The teacher later admitted it was her way of coping with their behaviour, but some students saw it as a punishment. A few students also complained about the teacher's management style. That was hard to hear.

Step 3 We then 'brain*waved*' suggestions for change (I don't like the term 'brain*storm*'). With some of my classes I have used the term 'surfing the brain space' (STBS).

At this stage it's normally helpful to just list (or have a student recorder list) the suggestions on the chalkboard. If they are outrageous ('Get rid of the teacher') then a clear, brief, firm reminder of the no-put-down rule is enough. Avoid over-servicing silly comments or gratifying their attention seeking (we can always follow up with such students later).

I emphasised, and my colleague joined in, that we were looking for ideas that would help us all to treat one another with respect, to learn well and most of all to enjoy our time together in music. 'We're not saying it can always be fun, but we are saying we'll work hard to improve things to make it as enjoyable as possible—and we need your help.'

The need to have some fun and freedom are (according to Glasser 1991) basic needs. This is an interesting concept, because if teachers ignore this fundamental aspect of 'social belonging' children will easily find their own versions of fun!

Step 4 We then went over the fairly long list of suggestions and referred from time to time to their original concerns and ours. The solutions that best fitted everyone's needs were written on the chalkboard. One of the suggestions was to do group work and we discussed how best we could form the groups and how we could blend instructional time with group work time. It was a valuable meeting and the students certainly saw *our* perspective as teachers and we too acknowledged and took seriously the perspective of the students.

The outcomes we all agreed on were:
- less chalkboard work and filling in sheets
- a reappraisal of class rules and consequences
- no group detentions (an early recommendation)
- no shouting or slanging matches (we'd remind them of the fair rules, which would now be published)
- more group work
- another meeting in a week to review how we're going, then a meeting in three weeks and then once a term
- more positive feedback and encouragement ('Be more positive . . . ' and 'OK, let's see if we can work that both ways')
- respect cues for getting teacher attention and support.

We added a few extras ourselves such as possible afternoon teas together and some short break times in longer sessions.

Step 5 We thanked them for their participation, showed appreciation for their effort and assured them that the issues they raised would be followed up. We noted, too, that the decisions made would be evaluated and their involvement in the process would continue.

Things did improve. There were a few setbacks and we did need an extra meeting to finetune a few things. What really helped was colleague support—classroom meetings of any kind are not easy if teachers haven't had previous positive experience to draw from or if they are not confident.

We also did some work on peer mentoring and reskilling (p 134). I could see the relational tone improve as my colleague took extra time on such things as personal greetings, remembering and using students' first names, changing negative correction to positive correction (p 72), inviting suggestions on units of work and respecting student opinions about music and music tastes. We did 'mutually participate' (*Coriolanus*, Act 1, Scene 1) and the effort and outcomes were worth it.

This approach—the classroom meeting approach—is used widely in schools to address issues of common concern. These can be anything from playground issues, teasing and bullying, to issues such as lying, stealing, cheating, put-downs in the classroom, homework concerns and noise levels. Many teachers at the primary level run regular classroom meetings (one a week) to enable issues to be raised, addressed and worked through.

The purpose of classroom meetings is basically to widen the students' view of who is affected and how they are affected by the kind of behaviours we are discussing:

- How might the teacher feel if and when . . . ? How do other students feel if and when . . . ?
- How does such behaviour (always be specific) affect learning and any of our basic rights at school? Who else does it affect? Our parents?
- What might happen if we choose this approach? How do you think it will change things if we do it this way? (Be specific.) Note that all class decisions need to be finetuned by the teacher at the close of discussion.
- Do the decisions made as a class about the class's behaviour fit in with the school's code of rights and responsibilities?

One simple test my colleagues and I use for student suggestions in a class meeting is the 3Rs test (Nelson 1987):

- Is it *related*? Are our proposals related to disruptive, inconsiderate behaviour, even bullying?
- Is it *reasonable*? If it can't be implemented, or if it's too impractical, costly (for example, build a new classroom or have a refrigerated air-conditioning unit in class) or unfair, we won't do it. But we can have an afternoon tea during our double-class period if we plan it well.
- Is *respect* kept intact? Does the suggested solution(s) keep the basic respect intact. Outcomes, decisions and consequences should not set out to hurt or humiliate anyone in our class.

Open meetings

The two basic kinds of classroom meetings we've used are open and closed meetings.

Open meetings give students the direct opportunity to share their ideas, feelings and needs. Seating can be in circle format or even formal. An open meeting can combine class dialogue or a written exercise. One of the standard written exercises I've used for many years is the 3W Sheet (see Appendix 4).

Each student is given a pro-forma exercise containing three key questions. These questions are explained prior to handing out the exercise. Students are encouraged to fill in the pro-forma exercise privately (the use of personal name is optional). Students answer the following questions on a separate sheet:

1 **What's working well in our class?** For example, are there any activities you particularly enjoy? Are there any lessons you can recall that went well? What made those lessons go well for you? Do you have an opinion as to *why* some things go well here? It is important to start with the positive questions first, otherwise students will just have a gripe session. Basically we're asking what they like, enjoy and feel works well

at the moment and why? This can include comments about the teacher, class, activities or environment. Students are reminded that if a comment about the teacher or other students is particularly personal they should focus on the behaviour and not attack the person.

2 **What's not working well and why?**
3 **What are some things we can change—and how?** What can *you* do to make this classroom a better place? What could we *all* do to make this classroom a place where learning, personal safety and fair treatment work better?

Students in a Year 6 class listed the following in response to a classroom meeting using the questions noted:

1 What's working well in our class?
   • I like school because of my friends.
   • We do some good things here, such as that project and what we did for science.
   • Sometimes the teacher does interesting stuff like . . .

2 What's not working well and why?
   • I don't like the seating here.
   • I think my teacher has favourites.
   • I don't think the teacher likes me.
   • I reckon the teacher shouts too much—so do most of the class.
   • We don't have enough free time.
   • There's too much boring work—like all the writing (referring to the writing of notes on the chalkboard).

3 What are some things we can change—and how?
   • It would be better if we could do different things, not just writing (this student's perception was unfortunately narrowed but she had a point).
   • Don't have favourites.
   • Examine *both* sides of the story when someone is in trouble (this from a very articulate and earnest student).
   • Some more free time would be great.
   • Get some better library books such as . . .
   • It would be great to have some outdoor climbing equipment.

Some teachers will use the format of the 3W Sheet as part of an open-forum problem-solving meeting. The students sit in a circle. The teacher goes through each question and the feedback is noted on the chalkboard as well as on a written copy. If this format is used it is essential that normal 'classroom meeting rules' are re-emphasised.

It is essential to always keep written notes on any classroom meeting so that effective reflection and monitoring can be made.

Closed meetings

Unlike open meetings, where students are encouraged to freely share their point of view, a closed meeting is conducted almost exclusively by the teacher.

The procedure for a closed meeting may be as follows:
• The seriousness of the issue is stressed by having a respected senior

teacher run the meeting with the regular class teacher. It is not, though, an exercise in reading the riot act. The teacher(s) will convey (in their shared communication) the seriousness of what is happening in terms of the behaviour of this class. The tone is firm but calm, and serious but not attacking the students. The emphasis is on their behaviours and how those behaviours are affecting basic rights and responsibilities. Students, in this kind of meeting, would normally be sitting in their desks (at their tables). Such a meeting has a formal tone.

- The teacher(s) outlines, specifically, what behaviours are causing concern. Wherever possible, brevity of explanation is the aim—not a long lecture or moral invective. We're painting a clear, simple picture.
- It can help to have the behaviours and issues of concern written up on a large clear poster (or several posters) attached to the chalkboard.
- Also have ready, for later in the meeting, a revamped and positively expressed set of key classroom rules with positive outcomes (and consequences for misuse of rights).

The aim of this kind of meeting is to do the following:
- Explain what the class is doing, what the class is like with respect to behaviour and learning, and the fact that the class is not working co-operatively. Point out how this affects fundamental rights and responsibilities (p 43).
- Re-establish the 3Rs—rights, responsibilities and basic rules. Make copies of this available later in the session as a kind of class contract.
- Re-establish some key behavioural classroom rules (as they fit in with school rules) and classroom practices. In subsequent classes these work practices can be outlined and monitored.
- Rearrange the class seating plan (p 27) if it is thought this would help.
- Outline key consequences including time-out if necessary (p 90). Point out that there will be no group detentions. Reaffirm the basic principles of YOYOB and ROR (Respect others' rights). Also, point out the benefit of working this way.

The key part of the meeting is to emphasise the following:
- 'We cannot allow the levels of noise and disruptions (noted earlier) to continue, especially the frequent talking while the teacher is talking. If there are any genuine complaints or concerns about the class, or how your regular teacher "runs" this class (or any of your regular classes), Mrs D and I are prepared to listen to your concerns and to personally speak with you. We will take your concerns seriously and seek to do something about them. There will be time later in this session to raise questions.' (An alternative is to conclude with the 3W Sheet, in Appendix 4, as a class-written exercise.)
- 'If you need help with your work or behaviour we can always give you some individual assistance. I know it's difficult to ask for help but that is what we are here for. We'll be having another meeting in a week's time. We'll see how the rules and responsibilities are going.'
- 'We have not contacted your parents—yet. This isn't a just a threat, folks. We believe *you* can help change the way this class works and that your behaviour, individually and as a group, is something you can sort out

without our having to hassle your parents.'

- 'I'll be speaking to several students—I'll let them know privately later—about the option of moving classes if some of them can't handle the options I've just shared. At this stage we don't want to split up this class.' (This option of moving students must be available at any year level where the feeling of malicious intent is resistant to change.) 'Thanks for your time everyone—I look forward to hearing how it goes.'

In the closed meeting it is important to combine an air of serious concern with formality, tempered with an acknowledgment of care and hope.

Mini-class meetings

Mini-class meetings are sometimes used where it is suspected that a larger meeting might prove a bit taxing.

I had observed how one Year 6 class had nearly destroyed any possibility of reasonable learning, not to mention their teacher's sanity! Half a dozen students frequently called out; many students talked persistently while the teacher was in active establishment and instructional mode, and several students wandered aimlessly during the on-task phase of the lesson.

I chose to withdraw three students at a time (while my colleague was teaching) and we sat in the corridor and quietly went through the key questions (noted earlier). I assured them we (the teacher and I) would follow up the concerns even if it took several weeks. Some of their concerns addressed playground issues, being blamed for 'stuff' they didn't do because they were in Year 6, and unfair treatment ('Luke gets blamed a lot but he doesn't always do what the teacher says he does; she doesn't always see other kids do stuff too!'), as well as noise level. I asked what we could do about this. 'We could try to be quiet,' was the sheepish reply.

After this exercise we took the findings back to the whole class for a more formal meeting to address the need to re-establish our class rules and routines especially noise levels (p 69).

Another variation is to use the 3W Sheet (p 33) within the 1, 3, 6 method. This combines individual and group focus. Students fill in the exercise on their own, then join a group of three other students (after ten minutes) and share their responses. After five minutes each group of three combines to form a group of six (or thereabouts) and five minutes later receives the feedback. Or the teacher can conduct the exercise individually and give the feedback at the next lesson (or the next day at primary level). The main point to stress is that we want the students' feedback.

Like any meeting format the mini-class meeting needs to be well planned with rules published and referred to during the meeting. Planning with a colleague can be really beneficial. Conducting the meeting with a colleague gives some emotional security and a chance for mutual reflection and feedback later.

I've also found it helpful, on occasions, to run a full class meeting in another room to emphasise that this meeting is special. We take the rules and our notebooks with us and return with our shared outcomes.

Meetings to deal with put-downs
Put-downs and teasing in class

Put-downs and hurtful teasing are an annoyingly common feature of a hard class. If ignored or tolerated ('Oh, they're always speaking like that') it can become the norm. I've been in classes where teachers have seemingly given up on frequent student use of 'idiot', 'stupid', 'dropkick', 'gees you're a dummy!', 'poofter', and so on. While much of this is sotto voce, in my opinion it is still unacceptable.

This issue can be addressed by having a clear classroom rule about respect, fair treatment and the use of positive language—'In our class we use language that helps people to feel good about themselves and good about others. This means no put-downs or slanging off at another class member'. This rule would form part of the class (or year-group) establishment phase.

It may also be helpful to run a classroom meeting to address the issue if a pattern of hostile and put-down language starts to emerge in the group.

Immediate reminder of the fair rule for positive language is important along with after-class follow-up. During one of my lessons last year a male student referred to a female student's head covering as a 'tea towel'. This student (a Muslim girl) was understandably and visibly annoyed.

Jeff had called across to her and said, 'You've got a tea towel round your head.' He grinned and enjoyed the little chorus of laughter from several boys. I looked at Jeff and said firmly, with a strong assertive tone, 'Jeff! [here I dropped my voice to a serious tone] that's a put-down. Our class is a no-put-down zone. That language is totally unacceptable.'

With behaviour such as put-downs and abusive language it is important to register to the student (and the class) the seriousness of the issue at stake. This will come across in the assertive (non-aggressive) stance of the teacher. Jeff responded quickly, 'Gees! I was just joking!' The sad thing is this is probably true. Jeff didn't see any religious or cultural significance in the girl's head covering—just an opportunity to have some fun.

'Maybe you think it was a joke, Jeff, but what you said was a put-down and that can hurt.' I blocked with my hand to both students and said 'I'll speak to you after the class.'
At the close of the lesson I asked Jeff and Mina to stay back for a few minutes. I briefly explained why I'd asked them to remain after class. The girl very quickly started to complain about what Jeff had said.

'Mina, if you're comfortable could you look at Jeff? He's right here. Tell him what he did and how you feel about it.' She looked him in the eye and explained she was quite upset because the head covering was from her religion and she had to wear it. Jeff looked at the floor, sheepishly. I asked Mina what she wanted to do about it. 'I just don't want him—Jeff, I mean—to say things like that.' I asked her if she could explain that to Jeff as he was standing right next to her.

She repeated it to Jeff, who replied that he didn't mean to hurt her and that he was just joking.

I asked Jeff what he could do to fix things up and assure Mina that she could feel safe—and respected—in our class. I reminded him of our school code about rights and responsibilities. He apologised to Mina and said he wouldn't say 'stuff' like that again.

I find it helpful in after-class chats to have the 'victim' and perpetrator (it's not always easy to sort out who is who sometimes) face each other and go through a basic process:
* This is what you *said* (or *wrote* about me or *took* from me in class) . . .
* This is how I feel about it . . .
* I want it to stop because . . .

It is then important for the teacher to invite the perpetrator to respond, but emphasise the right or rule affected and ask the perpetrator what they will do to fix things up or ensure that this will not happen again. It can be helpful to finish by telling the perpetrator to meet the teacher in a week's time to 'see how things are getting on'. This lets the perpetrator know you take the issue seriously. It can help to jot it down in the notebook (p 85**)** as an *aide-mémoire* and to indicate to both students that it will be followed through. This approach, at least, empowers the victim and directs the perpetrator to a commitment to stop this teasing, put-down or verbal abuse. More serious incidents will need to be handled through the school's due process for harassment/bullying. If a teacher (secondary level) hasn't got time for such an after-class meeting, it would be important to set aside a formal time to meet with the student.

A class meeting to deal with negative language and put-downs

A classroom meeting can clarify the issues for all; give a chance to air feelings, needs and concerns; and most of all educate for change in group behaviour. The procedure may be as follows:
* Have clear guidelines for the meetings.
* Plan ahead—advertise that next week there will be a special class meeting to look at negative language, put-downs and slagging off at someone in class (not a nice term but unfortunately common with some students).
* Use the conventions for classroom meetings (p 31).
* Print some key common put-downs used by class members on a large chart, for example, 'That's a *dumb* idea!', 'Gees you're a dickhead, poofter, slag, bitch, mole, dog-face' and so on. Students may not see these pathetic epithets as put-downs but just as 'fun', especially when they merely use them conversationally. Even 'stupid', 'drop-kick' and 'idiot' are hurtful to students, apart from the fact that it is inappropriate social language, and hardly contributes to a socially constructive environment.
* Discuss the use of put-downs:
  —How do people feel when such words are used?
  —Why is such language inappropriate?
  —Why do people speak this way—what are they trying to achieve?

—How does it affect our basic rights and responsibilities?
- Discuss other more productive ways of speaking that can convey displeasure, disagreement or annoyance without putting someone else down. For example, a teacher may say pleasantly and quietly, 'There's litter under your desk, Shane,' to which the student responds, 'So?' (said in a sulky snotty voice). Or a student may make a comment in response to a teacher's question in a class discussion and another student may call out, 'No, stupid. That's not it!' Discuss how the recipients (teacher and students) feel in exchanges like these and invite other ways of communicating disagreement or questioning another's ideas, opinions or perceptions.
- List suggestions of things to say or do, and choose those that fit in with our:
  —right to learn without feeling unfair or undue pressure
  —right to feel emotionally (as well as physically) safe
  —right to be treated with basic dignity and respect regardless of race, gender, religion, ability or disability.

  It can help to publish these communication reminders in a positive form as a class reminder about considering others when we communicate. There are some excellent examples of meetings that can address social skills in the book *Friendly Kids, Friendly Classroom* (McGrath & Francey 1993). See also *The Collaborative Classroom* (Hill & Hill 1990).

Class meeting and group establishment

One approach I've used is to ask the class a series of questions about effective teachers and students as part of a class meeting or formal class discussion. Have a couple of students record the answers on the chalkboard.
- Ask the class what makes an effective teacher. The answers come thick and fast ('knows how to keep order', 'has a sense of humour', 'is interesting', 'kind', 'fair').
- Then ask 'What makes an effective student?' I like this question because the answers indicate that students know what they need to do regarding listening, having relevant materials, taking turns, sitting 'still' and raising their hands as well as regarding attitude, working hard, being on time and so on.
- 'I then say, 'Well, it seems you know what an ideal class could be like. I'll do my best to be that kind of teacher [BDN]. Let's discuss some of the routines and agreements about working together that can help you do your part and help me do mine, so we can work effectively as a class.'
- The teacher then works on some basic classroom agreements (rules) and routines for smooth running of the class. These can be published and displayed when working with that class.

Another approach is to outline the essential rights we all have at school and how these rights relate to the classroom. Then ask:
- 'What kind of teacher would I need to be to enable those rights to be enjoyed?'
- 'What kind of students would you need to be?'
- 'OK, then, what class agreements will we need to enable us to work well together as a class?'

The last question can be developed through a small group activity with each group reporting back and seeing where the common areas of agreement are.

The class agreements are then published as a basis for ongoing management and discipline.

Last year we had a very difficult Year 7 and I was asked by the principal and guidance officer (school psychologist) to become involved. The main difficulty at the time was a large group of girls (nearly the whole class) splitting into 'gangs' and the beginnings of some physical violence. The decision was made to involve these girls in regular class meetings, which I ran very 'tightly', especially to begin with. Four of the very difficult ringleaders actually met with me once a week where I discussed their week and we talked about ways to deal with problems. I also had them on individual contracts monitored by their teachers. I think the sense of being listened to, even though I often encouraged them to understand the consequences of their behaviour and didn't agree with some of their methods, helped enormously. To start with, at meetings I tried some of the issues they all agreed on to begin the problem-solving process, for example a special area just for Year 7. There was a tennis shed to which, as members of Year 7, they felt they had special rights. This issue was non-threatening and non-divisive. As they gained confidence in the process and the guidelines we moved on to more 'touchy' areas. The classroom meetings had a significant impact in changing a volatile situation.

Colleen

Chapter 3

DEVELOPING A GROUP (CLASS) BEHAVIOUR PLAN

There is no failure except in no longer trying.

Elbert Hubbard, The Note Book *(1927)*

Pour out the pack of matter to mine ear,
The good and bad together.

Shakespeare, Antony and Cleopatra,
Act 2, Scene 5

A class plan or contract is another way of re-establishing and refocusing a class. It is simply collaborative agreement with the class on the following:

- basic and non-negotiable *rights* within the group
- basic *responsibilities* that correspond to one's rights
- necessary *rules* that give formal protection to rights and highlight one's responsibility
- *consequences* that follow from one's behavioural choices
- *support* for positive behaviour and for those times when students are struggling with their behaviour and may need a personal behaviour plan.

The dimensions below provide a framework that can be used at any age level (Figure 3.1).

FIGURE 3.1
CLASS AGREEMENT: BEHAVIOUR PLAN

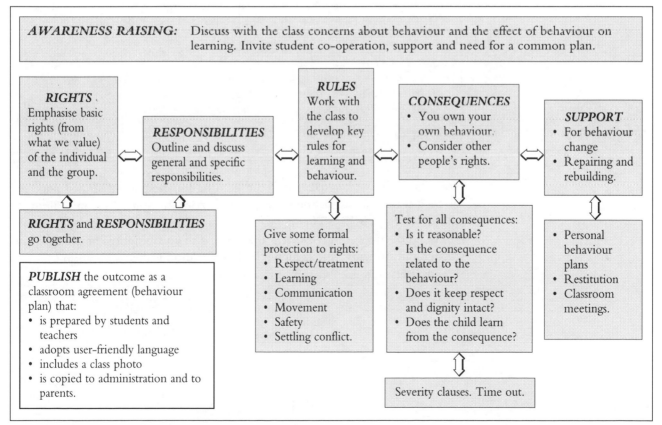

AWARENESS RAISING: Discuss with the class concerns about behaviour and the effect of behaviour on learning. Invite student co-operation, support and need for a common plan.

RIGHTS Emphasise basic rights (from what we value) of the individual and the group.

RESPONSIBILITIES Outline and discuss general and specific responsibilities.

RULES Work with the class to develop key rules for learning and behaviour.

CONSEQUENCES
- You own your own behaviour.
- Consider other people's rights.

SUPPORT
- For behaviour change
- Repairing and rebuilding.

RIGHTS and **RESPONSIBILITIES** go together.

Give some formal protection to rights:
- Respect/treatment
- Learning
- Communication
- Movement
- Safety
- Settling conflict.

Test for all consequences:
- Is it reasonable?
- Is the consequence related to the behaviour?
- Does it keep respect and dignity intact?
- Does the child learn from the consequence?

- Personal behaviour plans
- Restitution
- Classroom meetings.

PUBLISH the outcome as a classroom agreement (behaviour plan) that:
- is prepared by students and teachers
- adopts user-friendly language
- includes a class photo
- is copied to administration and to parents.

Severity clauses. Time out.

Through group discussion and ownership the teacher invites consideration of the common needs in the group and the common goals. Most students want a structure within which they can exercise appropriate freedom and power.

The teachers working collaboratively with the class demonstrate the following:
- The teacher takes the students' views and perceptions seriously.
- The teacher values the students' input by publishing a class agreement that can be used as the basis for teacher–student dialogue, management, conflict resolution, and repairing and rebuilding. For example, whenever students are behaving disruptively those students are affecting the due rights of the other students (and of the teacher). The students will be reminded of the right they have affected and of the relevant rule. They may have to face an appropriate consequence (within the class plan) but because behaviour is precipitated by other factors the teacher will offer behavioural support wherever appropriate. The teacher, with her class, works through the key stages (Figure 3.1) and then publishes the plan.
- The teacher gives a basis against which some reasonable measure for class behaviour can operate.

One of my UK colleagues has the following covering statement on her class behaviour plan (1994). I've adapted it slightly for publication here.

WELCOME TO OUR CLASS (ROOM 21).
- This behaviour plan has been discussed and developed by the students in Class XX. It is a record of how we behave towards others and wish others to behave towards us.
- The plan applies to all people who come into our class and will be used until the end of summer term 1994.
- The plan will then be evaluated and improved by the students and staff at the end of the summer term.
- Any new students (or adults) entering our classroom will be taken through the plan by a peer, who will answer questions and explain the rules in more depth.
- Our written rules are displayed on the classroom noticeboard.

Rachel 1994

Note the inclusive language and positive tone for the plan. This first page of the plan sets the basis for the subsequent sections on rights, responsibilities and so on (Figure 3.1). The key to a class contract, though, is not a published document in itself. It is the process of collaboration between teacher and students from which a higher likelihood of co-operation, responsibility and accountability can operate.

Basic steps in developing the behaviour plan as a 'class contract'

If a class contract is pursued as a way of re-establishing a hard class, it will be necessary to begin by sharing concerns about behaviour and learning within the class as it is now. If a class contract is used from day one, the teacher can pursue a *general* discussion on the need for a class agreement as a basis for teacher–student clarification about 'the way we will work together as a group'. Point out that we will be working on the issues of behaviour and learning in this class as a class group. Especially at senior levels, it is worth pointing out that it is not the teacher's job to control everything that goes on in the classroom.

I was developing a class contract with a difficult Year 10 some years ago, and several students argued that it was the teacher's job to 'control' us. I pointed out that as Year 10s they could, if they chose, walk out, scream, yell, work, sleep and so on. They choose to behave based on what they believe about their needs at school. We had an interesting discussion on the expectations of teachers and students (p 39). The students finally agreed the teacher's job was to teach, lead and guide but that we are all responsible for our own behaviour (p 19) in terms of its effect on others. This discussion led naturally to a spirited discussion on fundamental rights.

Rights

With any age group (five–18 years) it is important to focus on the basic, non-negotiable, fundamental rights we should expect to enjoy at school:

- *The right to respect and fair treatment*—it will be important to discuss basics such as personal space, treatment of school property and one's personal property, and even basic manners (such as ask before you borrow—don't just take). In this way a right is explored as the fair and reasonable 'thing' to do and also the behavioural expectation that goes with such a right.
- *The right to learn, without being hassled by others*—a discussion often follows on hands up, waiting turns and fair share of teacher time.
- *The right to feel safe and be safe*—this right addresses issues such as emotional and physical safety. All issues of bullying and harassment have to be dealt with from this essential and non-negotiable right.

A right is an expectation of how things ought to be—it is no guarantee things will be that way. This is why we need the corrective side of behaviour management—the rules and consequences.

The rights and responsibilities section of the class behaviour plan gives the class a structural framework against which responsibility and accountability are measured. Some class contracts outline the essential rights of the key stakeholders: students, teachers and parents (Rogers 1990).

Basic responsibilities

From upper primary level onwards students are keenly aware of their rights (perceived and real). It is important to point out that rights and responsibilities go together. Some responsibilities will be general (co-operate, share, act safely, do your best, and so on) and other responsibilities will be more specific (be on time, have relevant materials, and so on). By brainwaving with students and listing outcomes on the chalkboard the teacher can isolate the general and specific responsibilities.

Specific responsibilities often tie in with such routines as the following:
- Each class table group (primary-age level) will have a noise monitor to remind the members of the group about 'work-talk' and use of 'partner voices' (p 71).
- Movement around the room during work time is checked with the group leader.
- Leave your work area tidy (each table has a small, laminated reminder card, with the key tasks listed).

RESPONSIBILITIES

Responsibility is when you take control of your own thoughts and actions.

We have responsibility:
- to care for each other and ourselves
- to respect other people's work
- to set a good example for the school
- to treat belongings and resources with respect
- to control our noise level
- to keep clean the area where we work.

From a student behaviour plan. *Jackie, Grade 4 teacher, 1994*

Class Rules

Discuss the purpose of rules. Basically good and fair rules give some formal protection to one's rights. Rules are not mere impositions. If students have not had a decent discussion on rules at primary level, it can help to focus on the rules in our society—in football clubs, on the road, in swimming clubs and even at home.

You might discuss the following questions:
- Why do we need rules?
- What would happen if there were no rules to guide us, remind us and set standards?
- What makes a rule fair or useful?
- What sort of things happen when rules are broken?

Here are a few tips about class rules:
- Keep the rules as simple as possible.
- Make sure classroom rules tie in with school-wide rules.
- Phrase rules in a positive way, or at least have a balance of positive and negative aspects of the rules (for example, 'Hands up in class discussion— no calling out and no finger clicking' and 'Keep hands and feet to yourself—no hitting, no hurting and no play fighting').
- Keep rules few in number. The basic test of a rule is whether the rule focuses on the basic rights and responsibilities of the issue it addresses. Is the rule essential to social harmony and learning? With older students at secondary level, the term *classroom agreement* can be substituted for classroom rules if such a change is perceived as helpful.
- Avoid nitpicking rules (for example, 'No one leaves the room unless every piece of litter is picked up' and 'If you are caught chewing gum, all gum will be confiscated and thrown away').

- When publishing the rules, use inclusive language. For example:
  Our classroom rules are:
  —When *we* communicate we . . .
  —To show respect *we* . . .
  —Moving safely in *our* room means . . .

SAFETY IN OUR CLASSROOM

We take responsibilities for our action while at school:
- We use equipment appropriately and safely.
- We look after our property and the property of others.
- We wear only sensible clothes and safe jewellery, and tie back our hair if appropriate.
- We think about the possessions we bring into school and check that they are appropriate.

In some settings the rules for safety would need to be more specific (for example, 'Leave all toys and playthings—footy cards and so on—in your locker before you come to the mat' in lower primary). In one high school where uniforms were not worn, we put up a montage of photographs in each home classroom to indicate acceptable and unacceptable dress code.

In some classes there could be a lower degree of specificity because of the natural levels of consideration, thoughtfulness and social awareness. Many rules and routines have their highest focus and utility in the establishment phase of the year (p 61).

Students need to see the 'sense and sensibility' in the rules and routines in a classroom. Students have a keen sense of natural justice, and thoughtful rules will give a focus to that keen sense.

Use *key headings* to focus on the *primary* aspect of the rule. For many years now I have developed with students several key rule areas and discuss the necessary elements of the rule within those headings. Key headings are: Treatment/Respect, Learning, Safety, Movement, Communication, and Settling Disputes and Problem Solving (Rogers 1990).

By having key headings for rule areas a teacher can refer briefly to the rule, whenever reminding or correcting students—'Remember our rule for communication'. The teacher might also need to add briefly 'Hands up, thanks'. Having discussed and published the rules the class now has a framework within which to encourage responsibility, and give a basis for corrective (and supportive) action by the teacher.

Consequences

A consequence is the stated (or negotiated) outcome that relates to irresponsible behaviour.

When discussing consequences with the class, students will often be tougher, draconian even, in their views of punishment. Based on their backgrounds at home and school, they may see only the punitive side of consequences; some may even see consequences as a teacher or adult payback.

Firstly, discuss with the class the purpose of consequences. It can help to have a little question test to sort out from the students' suggestions those consequences that are fair and reasonable.

- Is the consequence *related* to the behaviour? For example, should picking up litter be a consequence for bad language? Would a written or verbal apology or a 4W Form (Appendix 2) be more appropriate? If students damage any school property perhaps they should do several jobs around the school as a 'civic-duty' consequence.
- Is the consequence *reasonable*? If students use art equipment inappropriately (for example, flicking paint on the window with a brush) does that mean they lose all rights to all art equipment or just brushes for the lesson? There would also need to be a follow-up consequence as well (for example, cleaning brushes and the window).
- Does the consequence *teach* students anything about their behaviour? What does a student learn from writing lines? At least with a 4W approach (whether written by the student or as a basis for teacher–student dialogue) students are challenged to reflect on their behaviour and come up with an appropriate consequence.
- Distinguish between a *rule reminder* and a consequence. In the first instance of forgetful or low-level disruption (calling out, talking while the teacher is talking or physical restlessness) students can be reminded of the classroom rule or routine. At times this can even be non-verbal. If the student is leaning back (annoyingly) during instructional time the teacher

can give a non-verbal signal (four fingers extended downwards). The first time such a signal is used it will be important to add the words (positively without any sarcasm), 'Four on the floor with your chair, thanks Jason.'

- Have a *severity clause* built into classroom consequences, such as time-out, within or away from the room. Students need to know that when their behaviour is *continually* disruptive they lose their rights in the short term (especially their right to stay in that room with persistently disruptive behaviour). It is essential to clarify this severity clause at any age level (p 90).

- Distinguish between *short-term* consequences, such as students being directed to work somewhere else in the room or having time-out if their behaviour is persistently disruptive or unsafe, and *longer term* consequences that will need to follow after students have cooled down and the class audience has gone.

- Most importantly a consequence needs to be applied with *certainty* and not intentional severity. Keeping the fundamental dignity and respect intact is a way of both respecting the basic treatment right and still holding students accountable for their behaviour. The message that we emphasise to the class and individual is that it's the *behaviour* that needs to be addressed and worked through. Tempting as it may be on occasion, the emphasis is not on teacher payback or revenge, for example 'Right, you could be out playing now, couldn't you, eh! No, you decided to leave a mess, didn't you? Now you're missing recess and it serves you right!'. This teacher rightly has the student stay back to clean up the personal mess, but instead of focusing on the behaviour so that the student remembers the certainty of consequential outcome the teacher is more interested in the severity message.

- *Link* consequences to repairing and rebuilding (support for behaviour change). The purpose of all discipline is to enable students to be reflective of, and responsible for, their behaviour and its effect on others. This is a challenging goal. If we want to help students in the future to be more self-aware and more responsible, we need to help them beyond the consequence so that they will repair and rebuild those behaviour and relationships patterns that are causing them problems. Some students will need work on individual behaviour plans to help them learn in a more specific, one-to-one, way more appropriate behaviours.

CONSEQUENCES

A consequence is what happens if you forget to use our behaviour policy.
A consequence happens when you choose behaviours that are hurtful to others' rights.

A consequence must have something to do with the behaviour and must be fair. A consequence will also be related to the problem and respect the individual.

- You will be asked to explain your behaviour to the person affected. You will be expected to explain to the appropriate person your feelings and reasons for your behaviour (the 4W Sheet—Appendix 2).
- We have a class response book where you can write an answer or response to your behaviour.
- If your class work is not up to standard you will discuss it with your teacher and you may be asked to redo it.
- If you disrupt the learning of others or affect their safety you may be asked to work away from others or take 'cool-off-time' and 'thinking time' (time-out, in or out of our class).
- Consequences can also be worked out during class meeting time. We will try to help with problems as a class. We will support the individual while trying to deal effectively with the problem. Class meetings are open to everyone. Consequences are recorded in the class response book, which we will use to follow through with the solution.
- If you forget your homework you get an extra day in which to do it. If you forget again you will do your homework in 'catch-up time', or do a set piece of work. Your parents may have to be contacted to support your homework plan.
- We can develop organised action plans to arrange individual consequences. We can also develop individual behaviour plans to help you change things for the better.

Year 7, adapted

Some consequences (such as those affecting safety, harassment, fighting, bullying and drugs) will be school-wide and non-negotiable. Many classroom consequences, though, will be negotiated with the grade teacher, based on the principles noted earlier.

Support for behaviour change

Support for behaviour change involves behaviour planning with students. This is addressed fully in Chapter 7.

Regular use of class meetings at primary level is an important feature of supporting positive behaviour and keeping the class plan on track.

Once the class plan has been discussed through its key stages (Figure 3.1) the class can elect a writing group to work with their teacher to write the class plan on the basis of the following principles:

- Adopt user-friendly, simple language relevant to the age group (see boxed material on consequences).
- Keep the overall emphasis positive where possible.
- Include class drawings and a photo montage on the cover and through the text to personalise the plan.
- It can help to have older students and the teacher sign the last page of the plan under the heading: 'Our class has discussed, drafted and edited this behaviour plan and we agree to use it.'

It can also help the home–school support process if a copy of the class plan goes home to each parent from that class. Of course, the teacher would need to have a covering letter, supported and countersigned by the principal, explaining the purpose of the plan and how it fits in with school-wide policy (Rogers 1995).

It is important that relieving teachers get a copy of this class plan (it normally runs to about 6–8 pages with pictures and photos included). Key aspects of the class plan can be recorded on classroom posters to set the class tone for the establishment phase of the program. Some schools run a parent information night where the common (school-wide) philosophy and practice of classroom behaviour plans are outlined for parent discussion and feedback.

It is also important that students and parents see the positive benefits of the class plan in terms of what it is trying to achieve. This includes the welfare and well-being of all the participants, the challenges to responsibility, and the positive outcomes in learning and behaviour.

The consequential chain

Students need to learn the consequential chain and how it operates, for example: class teacher ⇨ co-ordinator ⇨ principal. In *serious* cases all behaviour is directed to the principal and parents are notified, but the grade subject teacher is always involved in some way in the consequential process, even where the student is suspended.

As a part of the classroom contract session the teacher(s) will explain that consequences have *degrees of seriousness*. You could say the following: 'If you have been reminded of the relevant rule, or given a simple (fair choice) or a fair direction, remember that what we're seeking to do is to help you take ownership of your behaviour and consider others' rights. If you make it difficult for students (or the teacher) to feel safe here, to learn (or teach) or be treated with respect, one of several things will happen:
- You will always, always, be asked to stay back and meet with me (or sometimes another teacher) to explain your behaviour and sort out ways to change things for the better.
- In class you may be asked to work away from others in the room (or even just outside the room).
- You may be asked to take 'cool-off-time' and 'thinking time' in the class, away from others, or even just outside the class.
- You may be told (not asked) to leave the room for time-out in another room.

'You see, as your teacher, I cannot allow any of you to hurt others, or behave in ways that make it very difficult for others to learn or for me to teach.'

Developing class rules by discussion

Class rules can be developed by discussion. Using the key headings noted earlier (p 45) the teacher directs students to suggest the essential elements for each rule in the following way:
- Students work on their own, listing key aspects of rule areas such as communication, respect and movement.

- After 10 minutes the students work in pairs and note similarities and differences in their responses.
- Students then work in small groups of six for 10 minutes to note under each heading the common agreements of each group member.
- The teacher calls a halt on discussion and a reporter reads out (group by group) what the common aspects of agreement are for each rule area, and this is recorded on the chalkboard under each rule-area heading.
- Students then work in five or six groups to draw up and illustrate the rule cards.

DEVELOPING A CLASSROOM BEHAVIOUR MANAGEMENT PLAN: ONE TEACHER'S STORY

My teacher-centred approach was not going to work with this class! Their social skills were not strong. It was pretty obvious that I had to change the group dynamics as well as address the issue of poor social skills. I believe that the success that I had with this class was largely due to establishing more positive relationships with, and between, the students so that they valued what we were doing—not an easy task with a difficult group that I saw only once a day for forty minutes.

I started by looking closely at what I was doing. *I* was also a part of this group—a group I had to work with for the year. It was vital that I made a difference. Until the class could accept each other and develop a more positive, supportive classroom environment we would achieve nothing.

I put myself into their shoes. I tried to anticipate what discipline problems I would encounter the next day. I planned how I would handle each problem and even rehearsed what I would say. I also had an exit/time-out plan in place that I had developed with the assistant principal (p 92).

I spent as much time planning my discipline plan as I did the content of the lesson. When problems occurred I wanted to be able to deal with them in a manner that reduced stress.

It was essential that the class own its behaviour. I was totally honest with the students. I told them that I was really unhappy with how we were functioning as a class and that on several occasions I had shed a few tears after the lesson. I explained that I was under a lot of stress and we needed to address what we were doing—a brave thing to admit to a Year 9 class! The discussion that followed focused on how we liked to be treated and the rules we wanted to put into place to ensure that each one of us felt valued.

With this difficult class it was obvious that I needed not only to concentrate on social skills but also to ensure that the material we covered was interesting, relevant to them and enabled them to realise some success. I strongly feel that the development of relationships is an important part of behaviour management plan, as is catering for the needs and learning styles of students. It is not just a case of having a good discipline plan. Co-operative learning experiences were also invaluable in helping me establish positive relationships.

In coping with a difficult class I needed support from my colleagues, and at first it was not easy to discuss my problems. I received a lot of help from an assistant principal as well as a teacher who had 'rescued' me on several occasions when it all became a bit too much. I now tell my story as much as possible to encourage others who have difficult classes not to be afraid to admit it. As an experienced teacher it can be hard, but I found that many others were then prepared to discuss their problems with me and help me as well.

We were able to turn things around using a 'recipe' of a carefully thought-out discipline plan, the establishment of rules, routines, responsibilities based on valuing each other, relevant and interesting programs and, above all, a sense of humour and senior staff support.

Once the students could see that I was a part of the class and was interested in them and the youth culture, we were off first base. It was hard work developing social skills and positive relationships in the room, a well thought-out discipline plan, and interesting lessons catering for individual needs. However, my teaching became far less stressful and, by the end of the year, I was actually enjoying the class. The end-of-the-year class barbecue and the flowers from the students said it all.

An alternative for the last two points opposite is for the teacher to take away all the suggestions from groups and report back the common outcomes at a later stage. This is more appropriate at secondary level where a teacher is constrained by time. One of the common complaints of some secondary teachers is that this kind of group process takes away too much time from class lessons. However, the initial time invested in developing a full–class contract/behaviour plan is worthwhile in subsequent lessons.

Some teachers take a majority vote on rules and consequences, with the essential caveat being that no class rule can contradict fundamental rights or any school-wide rule.

Step 1: Personal review
- How should I start?
- Where should I start?
- Am I prepared to change from a teacher-dominated approach? Will this threaten and weaken my authority and control?

Step 2: Clarifying the issues
- Identify the problems.
- What behaviour do I consider to be disruptive?
- How often do disruptions occur?
- How do I react to disruptions?

A tape-recorder became my best friend for a week. I recorded several of my classes and identified the following problems:
- overreaction to minor disturbances, often leading to a win–lose argument
- some students treated differently from others for the same misbehaviour
- teacher-imposed discipline—student ownership of behaviour not apparent
- too many instructions at once
- lack of social skills in a number of students
- same misbehaviour occurring *every* lesson
- no clear class expectations—goals/aims often not discussed
- teacher indecision
- many teacher commands; few teacher requests
- no group cohesiveness; poor working atmosphere
- lack of assertiveness by teacher
- students often removed from room—no follow-up

Step 3: Action planning
- I read as much literature as possible relating to the issue of behaviour management, for example: *You Know the Fair Rule* (Rogers 1990), *Decisive Discipline* (1989) and *Behaviour Management—A Whole-School Approach* (Rogers 1995).
- I talked to my colleagues about concerns and looked for ideas, strategies, approaches and support.

Step 4: Action
- I noted misbehaviour in each lesson and how I responded to each instance.
- I planned my approach to similar problems I expected next lesson.

- I discussed *exit-from-the-room procedure* for serious disruptive behaviours. The discipline problem was not to be handled by the assistant principal or year level co-ordinator, with the exception of fighting, but was to be dealt with by me at more appropriate stages. The 4W Form was to be completed by the student (see appendix p 162).

Step 5: Class discussion
- Classroom expectations, rules and consequences were discussed with the class. The rules were clear and expressed positively wherever possible.
- How our rules matched school policy was also discussed.

Step 6: Discipline
- I started by choosing behaviours I would tactically ignore, and used non-verbal messages and simple directions.
- Over time, I gradually used other behaviour management approaches that focused on positive correction and encouragement.

- I ensured that all problems were followed up.
- I found it essential to reinforce positive behaviour once a disruptive student was back on-task.
- I was continually working on co-operative learning approaches to develop more group cohesiveness.

- Initially it was time-consuming but now considerably less time is spent dealing with disruptive behaviour.
- Teacher stress and frustration have reduced considerably, and a more positive, respectful classroom behaviour has been created.

Roxanne

Chapter 4

DEVELOPING A CLASS BEHAVIOUR PLAN USING GROUP REINFORCEMENT

A major purpose of behaviour modification is to change the child's world into one where appropriate behaviours are naturally reinforced. The teacher needs to intervene at first, but once the world has been changed, the situation should ideally be self-reinforcing.

Biggs & Telfer (1981)

Introduction

With very disruptive classes where a significant number of students seem to be constantly off-task, unfocused, loud, fractious and so on, it may be helpful to restructure the whole class using *group reinforcement*. Rather than setting up individual reinforcement programs with individual students, the teacher restructures the class into mixed-ability groupings. These groups are encouraged in positive academic and social behaviours by the use of systematic reinforcement. An individual's behaviour can benefit the group and vice versa and is selectively reinforced by the allocation of tokens, which are traded for *rewards* (as the students see it). It is not an elegant educational philosophy but as a short-term refocusing plan it can enable the kind of success that regenerates positive teacher and student relationships.

I am aware, of course, that to include any form of behaviour modification suggestions one risks the simplistic objection that one is merely interested in ends. Not so. Any educational and management approach is replete with values and ideals. It is my view that any method that diminishes a person should be called into question or not used at all. This view comes from what I value about people. I do not believe one can (or should) reduce complex human behaviour to stimulus and response, or some facile reductionism that says by simply applying conditions at A we can produce outcomes at B. Utility is no proof of value.

My purpose in including group reinforcement is to demonstrate that, with the students' full knowledge of what is happening, a class can refocus on positives and begin to celebrate group and individual effort in learning and behaviour. The rewards that form a key part of this selective reinforcement are a way of motivating a disruptive class. They are a means of acknowledging and affirming those behaviours that benefit the group and that are considerate of mutual rights. In time that affirmation and acknowledgment should be normative to teacher leadership. With group reinforcement a *process* is structured to enable that normative outcome. Whenever I've used this approach it has been in open discussion with students and never as an end in itself, but as a kind of 'social circuit breaker'—a *means* of changing the power brokerage in the room and utilising it for the benefit of all. With many groups I finish the program after several weeks and run a classroom meeting to discuss the lesson learned, the changes observed and future direction of the class (p 33).

There are countless studies showing that task performance, positive reinforcement, group motivation and positive behaviours can be enhanced by group modification (Brown, Reschly & Sabers 1974). One study with a 'head-start' classroom (in USA) showed that group reinforcement at infant-age level significantly reduced the incidence of aggressive behaviours (hitting, biting, pushing, shoving and kicking). This study combined group reinforcement with time-out procedures. Any act of aggression was immediately associated with time away from the group using in-class time-out (physical separation for cool-off time) where students cooled off for three minutes, with an audible timer to signal for teacher and students their readiness to rejoin the group (p 90).

The 'reward' cycle operated on an hourly basis, with all groups (of four) having the opportunity afresh each hour to see their efforts rewarded. The key to this program was that if one group member was aggressive or significantly off-task, the whole group lost the extrinsic reinforcement for that hour (Brown, Reschly & Sabers 1974, p 415). This program was tied into a positive class explanation of rules and the process. The reminder was given each day that the reinforcement process was in operation. Ideally class groups ought to work co-operatively without the inducement of rewards. We have found, however, that some groups of students need this reinforcement stage, initially as a precursor to co-operative group work. The overall aim of any reinforcement program is to fade out the extrinsic modification by the teacher to allow the classroom to operate under naturally occurring co-operation.

The process

This program relies on the use of basic behaviour modification principles and pure novelty to refocus the group. I have adapted this approach from McCarthy et al (1983); Brown, Reschly & Sabers (1974); and Barrish et al (1969).

My colleagues and I have used the following approaches to refocus classes of five-year-olds and 15-year-olds back to calmer, quieter, more task-focused groups (Rogers 1990). As one science teacher said of the very difficult Year 8 group we had been working with, 'Up until now I haven't been game to bring out any equipment and do experiments! I couldn't have trusted them. Now we're actually starting to work together.'

Preparation

Before you explain the program to the class, prepare four large charts with bright, clear, colourful headings.

Chart 1

This chart contains the class rules expressed as behaviours. These rules may have come out of a brainwave session (p 44). It is important at primary level that the chart outlines the rules simply, clearly and behaviourally. The following examples are rules from a Year 1 class:
- Line up without pushing and shoving.
- Enter the room quietly.
- Place all toys quickly in the locker and sit on the mat.
- Put up your hands to ask questions (no calling out).
- Stay in your seats at your tables (monitor gets materials).

Chart 2   This chart is for leadership selection (used at middle and upper primary and secondary). Point out that when you select a group leader these are the qualities to focus on:
- someone you look up to as a leader
- someone who can help the group co-operate and get the class work done (without yelling or threats—this point is made verbally to the class)
- someone who can help the group work by the fair rules.

Chart 3   This is a chart with four or five columns in which to list each group leader, the members of the groups and the 'points' earned.

Chart 4   This chart contains the rewards available for points earned. These rewards can range (depending on age or group) from stickers, stamps, free-time activities (board games, computer games, extra reading time, a class game and so on) to a special class video. The points allocation ranges from 10 to 100. At 10 points, for example, each student in the group gets an 'energy enhancer' (a dangerous jelly bean!) and at 100 points there is a class video.

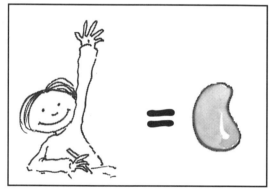

The points are always allocated to the *group* even if only one member of the group is doing the right thing at the time. In this way the group reinforces the individual and vice versa. The number of points corresponds to the effort applied by the group over time.

Note: Before embarking on any behaviour modification activity using rewards (especially edible rewards) check with your team leader or with administration. Some schools have strong philosophical/educational reservations about 'reward technologies'. Some schools will allow rewards such as free-time activities but no edibles, so it is worth checking in advance. Some teachers discuss with the class what special activities they would like to do and these are listed as behaviour enhancement outcomes (BEOs) or rewards.

Formation of groups

You could introduce the program to the group in the following way:

- Share with the class your concerns about class behaviour and learning but keep it brief. It may help, with older students, to have the issues/behaviours listed. Outline the changes you would like to make with the class: 'We're going to be working in groups over the next four weeks. We will need five teams of five (or six) students and we will need five (or six) leaders for these teams.' Have a bright heading on the chalkboard: 'Our classroom teams'. Underneath have Chart 2 (points for leadership selection) and Chart 3 (team groupings). This stimulates initial interest.

- For the selection of the leaders, outline the qualities of a leader (refer to Chart 2). Hand out slips of paper on which students are to write the names of two students they think would make good leaders (someone they would take notice of, listen to and respect). Tell students to write down one name if they can't think of two. I have had students ask if they can put their own name down! I explain that it is a choice about *others* in the group and say, 'If others believe you're a good leader your name will soon show up.'

- Collect the slips and note the names recurring most often. These will usually synchronise with your own views of responsible leaders. At lower primary level the team leaders are chosen by the teacher and the team members allocated by the teacher. While organising leaders from the 'secret ballot', give the class some busy work. It can even be a sheet or two of suggestions on how to improve our class (Appendix 4).

- Write the names of the five or six leaders on the group chart. Invite these leaders to come to the front of the classroom to privately select their team members (one at a time) from the class list until *every* name is selected. Do this 'privately' at the front of the room, to avoid public selection and the shame of being chosen last. At lower/middle primary level, team members can be allocated by random selection of names out of a container or the teacher can allocate group members to guarantee mixed ability. I have found it helpful at upper primary and secondary levels to brainwave with the class how they could form themselves into five or six groups smoothly, without hassle. We then select the most helpful idea and set them to it. From the outset it is important to invite the co-operation of the group (our ongoing goal).

- Read out the teams (there will be a few cheers—let that go). Call for group attention (p 68) and ask the groups to organise themselves to sit in teams. I've found it helps to have a large poster attached to the chalkboard showing where each group will form itself with tables/desks. Allow five minutes for each team to do this quietly, considerately and co-operatively. They can receive points for their effort. The restructuring of the class group into small groupings/teams changes the power dynamics of the group. With the behaviour modification process, the groups (and replaced powerbrokers) now refocus their attention on benefiting group welfare.

The 'reward' system

You can now explain the 'reward' system (behaviour enhancement outcomes—BEOs):

- Once the class is settled into its new groupings (five minutes at most) explain that points can be gained by the groups and as these points add up they can be traded for a range of BEOs or 'rewards'. Go through the list of rewards briefly. If *all* groups get to a common target, for example 500 points, the whole class can have a class treat. This could be a video as a class (from teacher selection, not an open choice) or an excursion.

- Point out that groups can *gain* (avoid easy use of the word 'earn') points as a group, or individuals can help their groups gain points by :
  —lining up without hooning, pushing and shoving
  —settling in their group quickly and quietly
  —working by the fair rules
  —co-operating in their group
  —leaving their area clean and tidy
  —reducing working noise levels.

- Initially allocate a point for all efforts and then, as the lesson progresses, give the points for extra effort. Be more discriminating. If any student complains point out, calmly, that the teacher is the referee, and that 'hand up', or 'lining up quietly' is the fair thing anyway. If a student is really objectionable either take a point off the team's score (the group will apply reflective group pressure) or point out (calmly, briefly) that this behaviour is not helping the group to gain points. Be careful not to take too many points from a team's daily score as it slows down motivation. It is better to say, 'You could have gained points if . . . ' and leave it at that.

- Make sure each group gets to at least 10 points in the first session. Observe all their efforts.

- If a few students object and say, 'You're bribing us' either agree or rephrase it, saying, 'Actually we're going to be enjoying behaviour enhancement outcomes. You'll see.' Also, point out that the teacher has the final say in points allocation—like the umpire.

- The giving of points on the class chart is the primary reinforcement. The secondary reinforcement is the group's acknowledging the efforts of their peers and later the BEO itself. When putting up the points, do it casually, without big fanfare, for example 'Craig, you've got your hand up—point for your team.' Leave it at that. Don't thank him—just briefly acknowledge.

The process in operation

The lesson material doesn't need to change *per se*. When using this approach, though, some teachers will set up special group activities to enhance group co-operation.

Many teachers have commented on how it has changed their perspectives as teachers. They start looking for the positives in their students, not just the negatives. As the teacher becomes more positive, the class tone changes as the students perceive themselves differently. I've had classes say they actually start to enjoy their work.

The normal discipline (including use of time-out) still operates within the program. It is important that any student's attempt to sabotage the program be dealt with swiftly—either immediate time-out (with positive follow-up) or allowing the student to work separately. In a Year 6 class one of the boys refused to join a group and so I had him doing all his work separately, away at a desk of his own. I gave him the choice of joining a group, at any stage, saying, 'Just let me know.' He joined a group in the second week.

It is also important that the teacher reserves the right (as umpire) to change any leader who is not keeping to their 'job profile'. This would normally follow a private discussion, after class.

Some teachers enhance the points allocation by having an audible timer go off at random times during the session. The group most on-task at that point (umpire's decision) can gain points too. Other colleagues have a tape-recorder going that gives out a random signal every three to five minutes. The class soon gets used to it.

Do not let students allocate points on the points chart as it can easily get out of hand with a feisty group. Only the umpire allocates points. Some teachers keep the points tally hidden from the students. I like to keep the points chart visible. I work hard to see that no one group gets too far ahead of its rivals.

Behaviour modification at lower primary level

Most of the guidelines noted earlier are relevant not only at primary level but also at lower primary—kindergarden to Year 3. At the lower age level:
- The grouping of the students is directed by the teacher as is the allocation of the leader.
- Students in each group have a badge with their group motif (colour, animal name, plant name, but not a football name).
- The allocation of points can be tied in with other activities such as the noise meter (p 71).
- It can help to have the points allocated on an hourly basis so every group gets some chance of scoring. Special effort rewards can be allocated for high scores. To enhance a *whole-class* ethos, as well as a *group-by-group* ethos, the group points can be tallied into a whole-class allocation so the whole class gets a reward when the whole-class tally reaches a target of, say 100 or 200 points. The target has to correspond to the working currency you set up at the outset. This group-points program has also been widely and successfully used at secondary level.

One novel approach at lower/middle primary is the group journey, where each group has a poster with a drawing of its car (different coloured car for each group corresponding to the colour of the group badge). The object of the game is for each group to fuel its car for the journey. The fuel is the points gained by the group's effort. As the cars get to 10 (fuelled by the 10 points gained) each group member gets a jelly bean. When the group gets to 25 points, each group member gets a sticker (it may take a couple of hours to get to this stage in the journey). The motivation is primarily in the fuelling (allocation of points) and the members' interpersonal encouragement. At 50 points the group can finish five minutes before the end of the period and do an activity (quietly) of their choice. At 100 they can try the balloon game (p 58).

Another novel approach is that each group has a poster depicting a basketball's journey to the ring. Each part of the ball's journey is coloured in (10 points for each part of the ball's journey) and there is a small reward. When the ball reaches the ring the individual group has a group game or activity.

One popular activity is for a member of the group to come up to the balloons fixed to the wall and pop a balloon. Each balloon has either a group game possibility inside (on a piece of paper) or a reward for each group member (a canteen voucher, a photocopy voucher entitling the students to make ten photocopies, a pencil for each group member, or a special game or activity).

The main thing about the rewards is to have:
- a 'currency profile' where students see the overall value of individual rewards
- emphasis on the effort exercised by students—not just the reward
- acknowledgment for the student's effort when giving points verbally.

Maintaining the program

- Keep the discipline positive. Use rule reminders (refer to the rule chart) or direct a question: 'What are you doing, Craig?' When he replies, 'Nothing!' say, 'Actually, you're working very noisily. What are you supposed to be doing?' If Craig says that he doesn't know, calmly remind him, refer to the rule, or ask his team to remind him.
- Use time-out for any persistent disruption.
- Tacitly ignore off-task behaviour only when appropriate.
- Speak to the group leader where appropriate (upper primary) and the leader can then refocus her/his group.
- Rotate group members during the course of the program if you think this would help.
- Increase the time needed to gain points and increase the points required for rewards, but discriminate in the allocation of points.
- Change the group leader once a week if possible at primary level and every second period at secondary level. However, if the groups are working really well, it may be appropriate to leave the leader in place or ask the group what it thinks.
- Fade out the program within six to eight weeks.
- Keep the tenor of the whole program positive. At the end of each day briefly remind the students what they have accomplished and the difference it has made.

- Run a classroom meeting at the end of the program to share what the students have learned, what they see as the benefits (or otherwise) and where we go from here. Discuss the benefits of the program beyond the rewards. Ask the students *what*, and *who*, really made the difference; they did.

Many teachers move on from group reinforcement to co-operative group activities with *naturally occurring* 'class rewards' that need no points allocation.

One of my favourite naturally occurring rewards with a difficult Year 6 was to have a morning tea once a week with monitors for tea, coffee and Milo and a plate of biscuits taken around by a monitor. Students were rostered to take orders, make the drinks and clean up/store away. They loved it—and we got plenty of work done.

Support from colleagues

If you have a very difficult class you may want to consider the group-reinforcement program but are not confident in planning and delivering the process. Utilise colleague support—there may be a colleague on staff who has used such a program. At the very least, having a colleague plan the program with you and help you set up the first session (day one is the hardest) will make you feel better. Invite a colleague to visit and observe a session, or part of session, and ask for descriptive feedback—this can help finetune the program.

Group reinforcement is not a cure-all. There are no guarantees that it will work with a hard class. However, I have had many, many teachers tell me that this program has been a great 'circuit breaker' with a class that was seemingly off the rails. It has rekindled teacher and class success, and with some teachers has saved their sanity.

> One of my American colleagues, who directs a behaviour clinic in Okalahoma, has used a reinforcement game with attention deficit hyperactive disorder (ADHD) students. The reward schedule is based on a simple board game where students spin a spinner and a piece is moved along a board. As they don't know what the rewards might be, this increases motivation and decreases dissatisfaction. The number on the reward card corresponds to a number on the board. Over 50% of the game cards provide activity-based rewards involving movement. Examples are: wiggle your whole body while counting to 50; act like a tightrope-walker in a circus; and have a game of Pictionary. The cards also give the opportunity to pick up a sticker or 'animal cracker'. Up to 10% of the cards give students an opportunity to pop a balloon (p 58). The chance to spin comes from points gained from their groups.
>
> The game is available along with a video program (McNeil 1994).

Students in co-operative working teams

One of my colleagues in a Melbourne secondary college has his machine shop run on the basis of teams or groups of three or four. The teams are of mixed ability and are rotated from time to time if necessary. They have rostered job descriptions involving monitoring and clearing away of equipment, and special afternoon teas from time to time. There is a tape playing music during the on-task phase of the lesson (tapes selected by students but no heavy metal). The tape is turned off for lesson transitions.

Each activity in the units of work is noted on a work card with easy visuals, all in a plastic folder.

The basic behaviour rules are discussed within the whole-school code on Day One, and the safety rules are published and placed near each machine. The class virtually runs itself. The students respond very well to the goodwill and trust communicated by the teacher. Goal-based learning and assessment and student co-operation are emphasised. This teaching method, when coupled with a positive and interesting classroom (workshop) environment, enhances both learning and social behaviours.

In a Year 7 textiles class we had each group of five students working on three key projects (with their visual/written learning cards) over time. In each group there was a noise monitor to keep working noise to partner voice level ('work talk' with no 'playground talk!'); a materials monitor, which meant that only a few people were moving around the room instead of 20; and group leaders who kept the group on-task and focused, reminded their team of the rules (where necessary) and kept the group supporting each other. To introduce the scheme the teacher (with a colleague for moral support) had a class meeting. In the meeting she discussed the present concerns about the class and then invited their concerns and shared her team proposal. She used the selection method for student grouping noted on p 55. The class rules and group responsibilities were published on bright attractive posters. The class had a celebration at the end of that term and regrouped for Term 3.

I have seen teachers at every level of education enhance student co-operation in the following ways:
- The classroom environment is attractive and functional (especially important at secondary level) with everything from seating plans to use of pot plants, curtaining, posters, work displays (even if it's taken down each lesson it's worth putting it up for that class) and use of visual learning.
- A teaching style that invites student opinion and co-operation, and conveys trust is adopted.
- There is a move from a positive establishment structure (Chapter 5) to opportunities for co-operative learning lessons. While it is not always possible to have a co-operative grouping approach in each lesson, it is important to blend teacher-directed learning with co-operative learning options to enhance socialisation skills as well as group learning skills.
- Classroom meetings are held to obtain classroom feedback. While this approach is used more often at primary level, secondary teachers are increasingly using classroom meetings to invite student participation, dialogue, problem solving and action planning. At the very least we can invite student feedback on aspects of our teaching and their learning, and the delivery of curriculum and services (p 33; Dalton 1985; Jones & Tucker 1990; Hill & Hill 1990).

Chapter 5

ESTABLISHING A CLASS

You cannot step twice into the same river, for other waters are continually flowing in.

Heraclitus, Fragments *(c 500 BC)*

When a group of students sits down for the first time in a classroom with a teacher standing 'up-front' there is a *group readiness*. This readiness is sometimes a testing time for teacher and students—especially with a hard class. The students are ready to see how, what and in what way leadership, teaching and learning will take place in this class; what the limits (if any) are; and how the teacher will communicate and enforce any limits. However challenging the class, there is a psychological and developmental readiness we can utilise to our best, and their best, advantage, BDN.

There are a number of routines, aspects of room organisation, procedure and expectations that are basic to day one and week one—the *establishment phase*. What we establish tends to have an initiating effect. If, for example, the teacher just allows the students to run into class, wrestle for the tables at the windows, call out, throw things and so on, it tends to convey a powerful initial expectation. If a class behaved like that more than once, it would be better to send for a senior staff member and do a joint settling/clarification than just battle on in the vain hope that things might get better. Of course, if we have a *disastrous* day one, it doesn't mean we can't turn things around, but it does mean that such turning around is harder.

I was discussing the establishment phase with a large high school staff recently and we decided it would be helpful if we reappraised our establishment procedures within, and across, faculties. It surprised some teachers that we were not sure what we actually did or said, for example:
- Did we line students up outside a classroom or just let them go straight into a class?
- How did we settle the class?
- How did we gain and maintain the attention of the group? What did we say and do to that end? Does it matter what we say and how we say it? If so, why? Why not? Were some ways of gaining group attention more effective than others? If so, why?
- Did we have seating plans or did students sit in friendship groups? Why? If we had a seating plan, what difference did it make to class attention and learning?
- How did we deal with typical early disruptions, such as students arriving late, students calling out, students with notices to hand in, students arriving with hats on and students chewing gum? Some teachers, for

example, felt it was important to object to hats and chewing gum, while others said it didn't matter to learning.
- How did we deal with disruptions to the lesson such as calling out, butting in, requests to go to the toilet, and so on?

What are we trying to achieve in the establishment phase? We agreed that basically we wanted to convey:
- a sense of order and purpose
- a positive tone in teaching, learning and social exchange
- some clarity on rules, the *rights* basic to those rules, and routines for the smooth running of life in our classroom
- the expectation that students are responsible for their behaviour, especially in how it affects others' basic rights, such as the right to learn without undue pressure, interference or interruption (by other students); the right to be treated with respect and dignity (whatever one's race, background or gender) including respect for property; and most of all the right to feel (and be) safe in this place (all harassment and bullying is an attack on one's right to feel safe and be treated with basic respect—p 43).
- our teaching and management style—a style that conveys respect with appropriate assertive leadership.

A number of basic aspects of classroom establishment followed on from these aims.

Lining up and entry to class

This sounds basic, but think for a moment how we settle 25 students with multiple energies outside a classroom (especially an outside demountable classroom on a cold day).

I walked down the corridor to the 25 Year 9 students outside Room 27. I could see at the front of the group, by the door, a tall boy holding another boy in a headlock. I asked him his name. He replied, 'Queen Boadicea!' and grinned. I looked him in the eye, in the hope this distraction and diversion would refocus him. I said, 'OK Queenie, let go of your mate, keep the hands and feet to yourself thanks.' He grinned back; turning to the group I asked them to settle, said 'Good morning' and directed them into the room.

What sort of things do we say to settle and initiate group attention in the corridor? It's worth thinking about some key phrases to use based on action verbs, for example 'look', 'settle', 'walk quietly', 'take' and 'sit on the mat a metre from my chair'. It sounds like dog training when put clinically on paper like this, but with a smile and hand gestures it can convey positive expectation and tone.

Consider the following:
- Do we go in first and have the students follow? Do we send half the students in and then go in, or do we let them all go in first? It's worth discussing this in relation to our age and subject needs, for example how do we set up appropriate entry to subject areas such as textiles, physical education and art?

• Do you greet your students on the way in or just wait for them to settle? At secondary level, especially upper secondary, there would be no lining up and a greeting *as* they enter would indicate a normal relationship. I like to stand by the door with a brief greeting to students as they come in. Of course, at primary level the teacher is already in the room before the first assembly bell.

Before the students actually go in to class it can help (at primary and lower secondary levels) to briefly remind the students of *expected* behaviours.

Positional placing

Where do we sit, or stand, while we seek to gain the attention of the group? How do we *wait* for the residual noise to settle? How do we signal that we want their attention and what cues do we use?

It is helpful to convey the impression and expectation that when we stand (or sit) at the centre and front of the classroom we require the group's attention. If we wander and pace the front of the room we may cause unnecessary (even involuntary) restlessness and visual tracking in our students. By *anchoring* ourselves and our words in that positional place we can build the association that when the teacher is here *group* attention is expected.

Of course, it is important to look calm and relaxed with open body language (not tensed up with arms folded or slouching), feet a little apart. If we look as if we expect the students not to listen and not to co-operate, we may get just that. Standing upright but relaxed, scanning the room and giving some tactical waiting time conveys expectation.

If we talk above their residual noise (and in difficult classes there will be residual, settling noise) we establish a possible norm that it is acceptable for students to talk while we talk. The waiting time may seem like five minutes, but it normally isn't.

As you scan the room, you show that you expect the residual noise to drop. A *non-verbal signal* can help as a preface to the brief waiting. The signal can be tinkling tapping on a small glass jar, rhythmic clapping, a raised hand or something else. I have a colleague who draws an oval on the chalkboard. He then scans the room and draws bright eyes on the oval shape (and turns to look at the students), then draws the ears on the now, emerging head (and turns again) and finally draws a smile. The attentive face on the chalkboard is now complete. It is another way of saying, 'Eyes and ears this way thanks.' He makes sure the face (in those first weeks) is gender inclusive and idiosyncratic each day!

If we use a signal to preface the waiting, we can then (after the five to 15 seconds) lift our voice just above theirs and step it down with the verbal direction, 'Settling down, [pause] looking this way, thanks [pause] and listening.' The 'stop, look and listen' signal still has mileage because it works (Barnes 1994) as a class 'norm'.

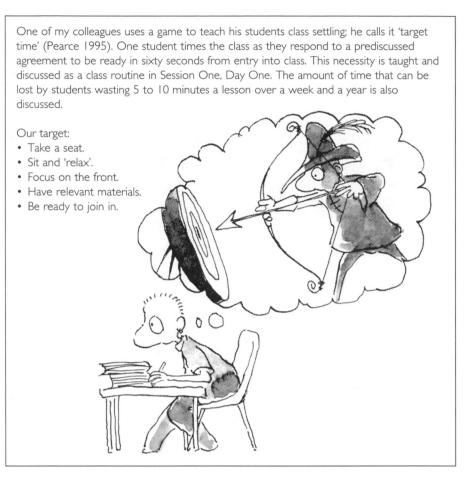

One of my colleagues uses a game to teach his students class settling; he calls it 'target time' (Pearce 1995). One student times the class as they respond to a prediscussed agreement to be ready in sixty seconds from entry into class. This necessity is taught and discussed as a class routine in Session One, Day One. The amount of time that can be lost by students wasting 5 to 10 minutes a lesson over a week and a year is also discussed.

Our target:
• Take a seat.
• Sit and 'relax'.
• Focus on the front.
• Have relevant materials.
• Be ready to join in.

It is also important to have a positive start to the session or day, especially a greeting and a get-to-know-you session on Day One.

After we have signalled the group's attention, we may have to briefly address any disruptions to group attention, for example a student who walks in late or students calling out. It is important to address these disruptions quickly and unobtrusively, with a refocus to the up-front learning, keeping the flow as smooth as possible. If we over dwell on these disruptions we send mixed signals to both the class and the disruptor (Kounin 1970; Robertson 1995; and Rogers 1995).

It is important to learn names quickly and keep using them in teacher–student dialogue. I've seen teachers talk to students without making any effort to use their names. For supply or temporary relief teachers it can help if they ask a reliable-looking student to draw a seat plan for them. I normally ask a student to do this on the way into the class. I have a prepared A4 sheet on which is written: 'To help me to learn the names of everyone in the class, please draw a plan of the room. Tables with first names will do. Thanks, Mr Rogers.' It hasn't failed me yet. The student passes it back to me and I can do a check, as well as use it during on-task learning time as I'm moving around the classroom. It is worth doing this each class period at secondary level as students may change seating positions each week if there is no set seat plan.

Clarifying cues for questions, discussion, attention and help

Some teachers prefer to deal with behaviour issues as they arise, while others prefer to clarify the basic rules and routines on Day One. Either way, it is important to plan how you will deal with calling out, several people talking at once, eating, lateness and so on.

It can be helpful to have a rule, even in picture form, indicating hands up, for example (p 44), and then discuss the hands-up aspect of classroom communication. Alternatively, you could start with a key heading, 'Our communication rule'. From a class discussion you could fill in the key areas of class communication. The same could follow for 'Our fair treatment rule' and 'Our safety rule'. Each rule could be accompanied by some pictorial aid symbolising the appropriate behaviour. Picture rules are very powerful at primary level, especially if students are involved in drawing them. By having a few simple rules teachers can refer (in their encouragement or correction) to 'our rule for . . .'

If several students are calling out, the teacher can give a class reminder, 'Remember our rule for asking questions.' The active verb 'remember' is more positive than 'don't forget'. As the teacher says this, they hold up a blocking hand, eyes scanning the room. A variation on this would be a (group) conditional direction, 'When you've got your hands up, without calling out, I'll answer your questions.' Similar language (and non-verbal signals) can be used when addressing an individual who is calling out. A pleasant, invitational tone will carry the meaning and it won't sound as though we're in contest or putting a student down. Then acknowledge a student with his hand up, 'Tim, you've got your hand up, what's your question?' If a student persists in calling out we will need to follow up with a chat about getting excited and 'jumping in' ahead of others. We can invite their co-operation (we don't need to punish).

By teaching and reinforcing these cues from Day One we set the tone for up-front teaching and discussion. In contrast, if we ignore or negatively correct ('Don't call out!' or 'Don't talk while I'm talking'), we set an unnecessarily negative tone.

Tactical pausing

Much of a teacher's intent and tone is communicated non-verbally (Grinder 1993; Rogers 1995). When correcting students we aid the registration of intent by adding brief tactical pausing between their name and the direction.

Two students are chatting while the teacher is teaching up-front. She looks at them and says, 'Sarjam [pause], Sarjam [pause]'—she has to repeat because he is not attending—'and Milan [pause], I can't teach while you're talking.' This describes what she sees as well as her need. That is sometimes enough. She may add a behavioural direction, 'I need you to face this way and listen [pause]. Thanks.'

The brief tactical pausing also allows take-up time (Rogers 1995) as the teacher brings their eyes to the whole class, resuming the lesson.

Cues for on-task attention

It is wearying for teachers to have several hands up, some clicking their fingers, to ask for teacher attention during on-task learning time; or the 'crocodile' line of Grade 3s, work in their hands, waiting and waiting for teacher feedback, and having a hair pull here or a little bored punch there.

We could use the routine/rule:
- 'Checking first with three students at your work area before you check with me.' Explain on Day One how they might do that. Discuss *why* and *how*.
- Number the hands, 'I see one, two, three. Michael, Jude, Chris, I'll see you in turn. Remember to go on with your spelling list [or whatever] until I come.' It can help to have a class understanding on alternative work to do in 'wait time'.
- Set up class mentors who can confer with students either at their own table or a spare area in the room. This approach can work at any year level.
- Some teachers use a teacher-help board (THB) at upper primary and secondary level where students can write their name and be assisted in turn.

The teacher-help board

The THB is a simple technique (a visual prop) that can be used in any class. It is ideal in such subject areas as art, textiles, information technology, manual arts and home economics. In these situations teachers often have their backs to students and there is frequent mobility by students during on-task learning time. Because of the nature of the subject area the teacher can hardly expect a simple hands-up rule.

The THB is made up of two charts. One chart has space for several names to be written consecutively from one to five. This chart can be a whiteboard or you can reserve a space on the chalkboard. The other chart contains rules on how to use the THB (Figure 5.1), for example **Remember** (before you write your name up here):
- Check the work requirement yourself. Read it and ask yourself, 'What am I asked to do here? Have I understood it? Where do I start? What do I need to do first?' This information can be on a separate poster.
- Check the work quietly with your partner, or check with three other students before me.
- Write your name on the THB, and I'll come round in turn.
- While you are waiting for me, carry on with the other worksheet (or class novel, spelling list, and so on).

FIGURE 5.1

> **REMEMBER**
> 1 Check the set work yourself.
> 2 Check with a classmate (remember 'partner voices').
> 3 Write your name (quietly) on the THB. Go on with your set work.
> Thanks.

The purpose of the chart has to be explained on Day One: 'It's your responsibility to consider my share of time for all. This is one way we can do that. Let's give it our best shot.' If students are abusing this system a thoughtful after-class chat may help (p 84).

Planning for transitions

I have been in classrooms where the transition between the up-front instructional phase of the lesson and the on-task phase is significantly unclear. In some instances students do not know when the teacher has finished teaching and when they are supposed to start the next phase, or (worse) whether there is an on-task phase at all.

Transitions need to be clear, with visual (on the chalkboard) explanations—steps, page numbers and noted examples—so that students don't start the attention-seeking whine, 'What do we have to do again?' Poor transitions can contribute to a significant rise in noise level, boredom or confusion. I've seen teachers hand material out *while* still talking, instead of completing the task explanation and getting a few key students to act as materials monitors.

Students without equipment

Teachers sometimes get into long, pointless arguments with students over not having pens, pencils, rulers or workbooks/paper and may even send students to a co-ordinator. Asking a student to get equipment from someone else can cause needless delays.

I find it helpful in secondary and upper primary classes to take a box containing pens, rulers, pencils, paperclips, name tags, chalk, duster, whiteboard pens and so on. The box is coloured and each writing implement (for students) has a tip of coloured tape to track it back to the box. My students know it as the 'yellow box'. I also take a pile of lined A4 paper. Being prepared helps to minimise unnecessary disruption. My rule of thumb for students is that if they forget (or do not choose) to bring required materials on three separate occasions (in close succession) we'll have to sit down and make a plan together.

Helpful hints

Here are a few helpful hints:
* Have a few extra sheets that have been photocopied from the set text for those students without a textbook or who have 'forgotten'.
* Have key tasks or task requirements (such as 'Page set out' and 'Five steps in writing a draft') published in a user-friendly form around the room. It saves repeating the familiar over and over. Have a class noticeboard with daily items/reminders. This caters for visual as well as auditory learners. I've been in classrooms where teachers have given all the instructions for a learning task/requirement in one teaching style alone—spoken (not

even the reference to page numbers was written up for visual learners).

- Have a tray for completed (to be marked) work with ongoing learning activities for early finishers.
- Have a simple pack-up routine and signal for transition to lesson closure. Teach the required routines on Day One and enforce them until they become routine. Make the routine the norm in the first few lessons and it becomes a group habit. It can also be helpful to give all group instructions or reminders from the one positional place—normally at the front of the room. This gives a familiarity of association.

Gaining attention

If students are not actually *attending* to the teacher and the learning experience, it is clear that little effective teaching can take place. Gaining and sustaining attention is not merely some starting technique. It includes the ability to build a rapport through having teaching and learning experiences appropriate to the age situation. I've seen, for example, classes at lower primary where all the expository teaching was oral/aural. There were no visuals, no engagement with the students by question and no involvement by a brief role-play up-front, not even a regular scan of faces and 25 pairs of eyes. If teachers are going to engage and motivate learners and learning they need to consider how to gain, sustain and focus group attention both in the up-front and on-task phases of the lesson.

Management skill has to be applied in combination with solid lesson planning and thoughtful use of the curriculum. Here, again, planning with colleagues will assist in motivating, and meeting the needs of, our students.

Teacher A teaches grammar to a Year 6 class. The students are restless and bored, and there is little application during the on-task time. The teacher has talked a lot and has used the text, but in a way that stimulates little interest or understanding. The rest of the lesson consists of examples of punctuation read out by the teacher.

Teacher B teaches the same unit, but begins by talking about a bicycle having a puncture, 'Who's ever had a puncture on their bike?' They discuss tool kits designed to fix punctures. The teacher goes from this to punctuation, and draws the tool box needed for punctuation with tools such as a full stop, comma, speech marks, question mark and the starting capital. He has several lively and relevant examples of text that sound funny and confusing without punctuation. He engages students as often as possible, and then sets them to work to use 'the kit' themselves. The kit is a worksheet naming the 'tools' and their usage. They then apply that to the task on the chalkboard, with follow-up tasks to come.

Of course, this is ten times harder with poorly motivated students and subject areas deemed a waste of time by some students (and even some teachers). I've been in schools where languages other than English (LOTE) seem to be rated as non-essential or unimportant and beyond the core curriculum. Some teachers (from other faculties) will even convey that view to students and not actively support subject areas such as LOTE. This is especially difficult for teachers who, for example, are already at a disadvantage if there is an anti-foreign languages mentality present in the community.

All subject areas need to be given credibility and support at faculty and staff meetings. Year heads especially should convey the appropriate status of subjects so their students can't simply hijack subject areas they think are useless.

Monitoring 'working noise'

My colleagues and I have found that it is important to *teach* and monitor 'working noise', particularly in classes with a reputation and in schools where classes are streamed (Rogers 1995). In 'bottom' classes behaviour and learning problems may be associated. In such classes we've found noise monitoring and feedback a useful way to teach healthy 'working noise' or 'work talk' (as one of my primary colleagues describes it to her Year 3 class).

The noise meter is a visual display of cartoons and a coloured 'signal' wheel to indicate different noise levels (Figure 5.2). The pictures need to be clear, blackline drawings, able to be seen from the back of the classroom. The four drawings indicate:

1   hands up (and listen when others speak, one at a time, without calling out) when we are on the mat—at upper primary level the picture indicates students sitting at their desks/tables with hands raised
2   partner communication/working noise/using 'partner voices' (Rogers, 1995, Robertson 1995)
3   reminder that class noise level is getting too loud
4   too loud—we need to stop and go back to partner voices.

The centre colour wheel signifies noise-level zone by colour (white = **1**, green = **2**, yellow = **3** and red = **4**). It is an ideal teaching activity for lower primary level for the establishment phase. White is for up-front instructional time, green is for on-task time, yellow indicates that the noise level is too high, and red signifies 'Stop'.

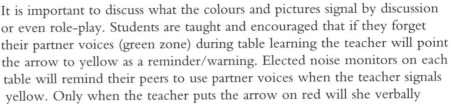

It is important to discuss what the colours and pictures signal by discussion or even role-play. Students are taught and encouraged that if they forget their partner voices (green zone) during table learning the teacher will point the arrow to yellow as a reminder/warning. Elected noise monitors on each table will remind their peers to use partner voices when the teacher signals yellow. Only when the teacher puts the arrow on red will she verbally signal the class to 'stop, look and listen'. She will then briefly remind them to stay in the green zone (and remember their partner voices). The whole activity is designed to encourage co-operation, keep verbal directions to the minimum (for example, yellow zone is a non-verbal reminder), and enhance visual non-verbal teacher reinforcement. It minimises 'Shush' and 'You're getting too loud'.

Some teachers link this to a points tally and free-time activities (Chapter 4) but it can easily stand alone as a means of establishing and teaching healthy working 'communication'.

I've used the noise meter, in modified forms, right up to Year 9. However, for upper primary and secondary levels I've used a simple chalkboard graph that gives feedback on class noise level during on-task learning time. The vertical axis has whisper zone at 2, and upper limit of partner communication at 5 (on scale of 0 = total silence and 10 = major migraine level!).

The horizontal scale has 0–30 or whatever the normal time period of a class is. The line is divided into three-minute or five-minute time slots. Every five minutes the teacher can quietly walk to the chalkboard to give feedback (non-verbally with coloured chalk). Peer pressure, we hope, will do the rest. Like the noise meter the graph needs to be explained and encouraged (in a fun way) as a way of helping us to manage class noise to enable positive learning. Points can be allocated relative to the class effort to manage their noise level and targeted to a score (say 20) that allocates free time (of, say, five minutes) towards the end of the class period, or the points tally (of 20) can be built up over two class periods.

Dealing with disruptive behaviour

It is important to consider how disruptions can be dealt with in the key phases of the lesson: entry and settling, up-front teaching time, transitions, on-task learning time and at the lesson's closure. Here we will deal with the up-front phase (when the teacher requires group attention and students are facing directionally the same way) and the on-task phase (when students are engaged in on-task learning in groups, pairs or even individually).

In the up-front instructional phase of the lesson

In the 'establishment phase' (as noted earlier) there is a group readiness—students are expecting us to exercise some leadership or control. After all they've had several years or more of adult discipline. They've also had a variety of management styles from authoritarian to *laissez faire*. We need to communicate our discipline style in a decisive but confident way if we are going to set a positive classroom tone.

Avoid talking over residual noise level. Teachers talking over or through students' chatter sends (at the very least) an ambiguous expectation of how things will be. It may be enough to use the tactical pause (p 65) or to give a general reminder: 'Several people are talking. Face this way and listen. Thanks.' Say this in a confident voice, scanning the eyes in the room, with relaxed but upright body language, blocking with the left hand briefly and beckoning (to the talkers) with the right hand once or twice as if to say, 'I expect you to do it, folks.' It is difficult to convey in print the powerful effect of non-verbal behaviour. John Robertson (1995) notes the following in the introduction to his book *Effective Classroom Control*.

> *Gestures, vocal variations, facial expressions can reveal a teacher's insecurity or boredom. Unlike words, their meaning is often ambiguous and can only be interpreted reliably if we have other information, such as the status of the speaker and what he is saying. Nevertheless, when there is any discrepancy between the meaning of the words being spoken and the non-verbal behaviour accompanying them, it is the latter which we take to reveal the real feeling of the speaker.*

Giving thought to language skill and our non-verbal signals will help consolidate our communication as teachers. The 'presentation of self' (Goffman 1972) is an important factor in behaviour management. If we look sloppy, indifferent, overly tense or anxious, and if our voice tone manner is characteristically off-hand, sharp or unnecessarily negative, those aspects of self will override what we say.

Non-verbal skills such as tactical pausing, positive eye contact, upright bearing, pleasant tone of voice (assertive when necessary), expectancy in one's voice and the use of gesture add up to a 'global' presentation that students can pick up very quickly (Rogers 1995).

Corrective language

The style of corrective language is important:
- Try using positive verbs or participles wherever possible: 'Do' rather than 'Don't' and 'Look this way, thanks' rather than 'Don't talk while I'm talking'. For example, 'Leave the windows for now, and face this way.'
- 'Damien and Ibrahim, look this way and listen. Thanks.' (In an up-front context) 'Thanks' contains a little more expectation than 'Please' when it's said positively.
- Try 'Hands up without calling out' rather than the simple negative 'Don't call out'.
- Use simple *descriptors*: 'There's paper on the floor' rather than 'You've made a mess down there' or 'It's noisy at this table' rather than 'Shut up here'.
- Use the language of 'choice' when appropriate (Rogers 1990). 'Yes, you can go to the toilet *when* I've finished this story.' Compare 'No, you can't go because I've just started this story.' The following are more invitational: 'When/then', 'Yes/when' and 'After/then'.
- Use inclusive language when giving group directions: 'In *our* class *we* have hands up without calling out. Thanks.' Then look for a hand that is quietly up and reinforce it quickly. 'Yes, Tim, what's your question?'

Class clowning and silly comments can be met with tactical ignoring (where appropriate) or with a repartee or a defusing comment where comfortable. Humour is a very powerful way to defuse and refocus attention away from tension, but it depends on one's personality and ability. It should not be confused with sarcasm or teacher put-downs.

The teacher needs to avoid unnecessary attention but, if given, give it briefly: 'That's not a helpful comment right now' and move on with the lesson.

If a student puts another student down, loudly, in front of his peers, eyeball the student. Use a firm voice and name the student: 'Jason!' Then drop your voice to a serious tone and add the clear statement, 'In our class we have a rule for respectful language' or '*That's* a put-down and that hurts. Our class is not a put-down zone.' Using 'That' indicates we are separating the behaviour from the person as it were. Follow up later (p 84).

I have a poster in my room when I teach to illustrate it is a no put-down zone (Appendix 5). If put-downs are common, it is worth following up with the perpetrator(s) and the victim with an after-class chat or even run a class meeting to address the issue (p 37).

In the up-front phase, management and discipline of any individual always has a direct audience of 25 (plus) students. It is important therefore to do the following:
- Keep the level of intrusiveness 'low'. For example, if a student is wearing a hat and the teacher wants to address the hat rule, a non-verbal signal is often enough. If a student is late, and the lesson has started, acknowledge the arrival, direct the student quietly to a seat and follow up later with the 'late pass issue'.
- Keep the focus on the behaviour or the rule, and avoid attacking the person, for example 'Jason and Kahn, leave the blinds and face this way, thanks.' In this case 'leave' and 'face' are behaviours you want to see, rather than merely telling them not to fiddle with the window blinds.
- Keep the direction or reminder brief. Avoid arguing. If a student tries the time-wasting last words, 'But he was calling out too', gently block the student or reframe what has been said by partially agreeing and refocus the issue back to the primary issue.

Gentle blocking refers to repeating the direction or reminder clearly (not aggressively), with expectation, and then regaining the flow of the lesson. For example:

Teacher: 'Jarrod, Karl, looking this way and listening, thanks.'
Student: 'We're not the only ones talking.'
The teacher repeats the same direction, briefly pauses and continues the lesson flow.

Partial agreement refers to a teacher acknowledging what the student says, briefly 'agreeing' and reframing it.

Teacher: 'Leave the window, thanks Jeff, and face this way.'
Student: 'But I need some air.' (He grins.)
Teacher: 'We'll organise the air later. Face this way, thanks Jeff.'
The teacher resumes the lesson flow.

However, if they continue with the disruptive behaviour, the teacher will clarify the immediate or deferred consequence: 'If you continue to talk while I'm trying to teach I'll have to ask you to work separately' (or 'see you after class').

Some teachers write the name of the student on the chalkboard as a public signal, indicating a clear warning that if the talking continues the teacher will put a tick against the name. The addition of a second tick means an after-class meeting or detention. With hard classes this method may well invite an unnecessary power struggle and should be developed only within a clear team approach and the backing up with consistent follow-up and follow-through of difficult students.

Following up students after class is an important process in establishing the certainty of consequential outcome. (This is explored in Chapters 6 and 7.)

Distinguish between short-term correction (what one can say in the immediate emotional moment) and long-term follow-up when the audience is not around and most of the heat has gone.

In the on-task phase of the lesson

Behaviour management during the on-task phase of the lesson can be more personal (because we are able to move around and alongside students) and more extensive in range.

If a student is chewing gum, the teacher can use a non-verbal signal to indicate the bin or an incidental question: 'Dave, are you looking for the bin?' I've often taken the rubbish bin to the student to invite co-operation.

If two students are talking loudly, the teacher can say, 'Dave, Karl' and signal non-verbally across the room, by making a volume turning-down signal with thumb and forefinger. The teacher could walk across and quietly say, 'Talk inside your heads *while* you're working.' Context and the student's age will modify our language but we need to consider the points noted earlier about brevity, focus on behaviour, keeping the language positive where possible and avoiding arguing or unnecessary confrontation.

Correction will vary depending on the situation.
- Correction may be as a conditional direction. Maria asks if she can do the next activity but she has left a mess on her table. You could reply, 'Yes, Maria, you can, when you've cleaned your work area.' (Note that 'area' is preferable to 'mess'.)
- Correction may be simple choices: 'Darren, I want you to put your basketball cards in your bag or you can leave them on my desk.' This is more invitational that snatching the cards or just holding out your hand. If the student protests that he wasn't looking at them the teacher can gently block or refocus by saying: 'Maybe you weren't, but put them

away in your bag and carry on with your work.'
- It can help to leave the student with a task-related direction, reminder or question after such a choice, for example: 'What should you be doing now?' or 'Carry on with your work, thanks Darren.'

Direct questions focus on the present behaviour or issue and invite responsibility, for example 'What are you doing?' rather than 'Why are you calling out' or 'Why haven't you started work?'.

A student is 'off-task' talking to a friend. The teacher has tactically ignored the apparent time wasting for a while, but she now walks across to the students casually and directs a question at them both.

Teacher: 'What are you doing?' (The teacher is not aggressive—just relaxed yet decisive in tone.)
Student: 'Nothing.' (said a little defensively)
Teacher: 'Actually you're talking quite loudly to each other.' (She gives some brief, factual feedback.)
Teacher: 'What are you supposed to be doing at the moment?' (Her tone is pleasant and her body language is relaxed.)
Student: 'We're not the only ones talking.'
Teacher: 'If other people are talking I can remind them.' (brief partial agreement) 'What are you supposed to be doing? (She refocuses.)
Student (sighing): 'Our project.'
Teacher: 'OK, carry on with your project. I'll come across later and see how it's going.' She smiles as she leaves them with a general task reminder.

Also, during the on-task phase teachers can sometimes call the student aside for a brief private word or even go into the corridor for a 60-second reminder. For example, Frank had walked to the bin with a piece of screwed-up paper. On route he tapped it on three students' heads. It created the effect he wanted. He walked back to his seat grinning. Should the teacher ignore this? There is a time for *tactical* ignoring, such as ignoring the sulky pouting face or whining while focusing on the behaviour that precipitated it. In the case of Frank, however, 'ignoring' would be seen by the other students as de facto acceptance.

The teacher called Frank aside, away from the other students, just outside the door. She still had line-of-sight back into the room. Frank sauntered over, face screwed up, and said, 'Yes—what do yer want?' In a low voice the teacher said, 'Do you know what you just did in class?' (The class realises she is 'disciplining' him.) 'I was just putting some litter in the bin,' moaned Frank. 'I didn't want to embarrass you in there, Frank,' she said, 'but you actually tapped three students on the head with the litter on the way.' Frank replied, 'Gees, I was just mucking around—they are my mates.' The teacher terminated the correction by saying, 'Even if they are your mates, Frank, in our class we keep our hands and feet to ourselves, thanks. Come on, let's go back in.'

I've had students say, 'You can't make me' or 'I don't care' or the insouciant 'So?'. In this case partial agreement can non-aggressively refocus. Rather than walk across and push the boy's feet off, or confront him with detention, we can clarify the consequences and heighten his choice: 'If you choose to sit like that, you're choosing to have me follow it up with you later,' or 'I can't make you, but if you continue with your feet up, I'll have to follow it up at recess.' If he replies, 'Don't care,' the teacher can say, 'But I do. We observe basic manners here—I'll see you at recess.' He then retorts, 'No you won't!' If he continues with what he perceives as counter challenge, use the back-up time-out plan (p 92). It will be essential, though, to follow up with this student (with a third party if necessary) at a later time.

I've been in classes where teachers ignore these small events (feet up, playful punching, gum chewing, loudness, throwing pens to each other and so on) so that in time there is a general noisy, distracted, unfocused 'culture' in the room that contributes to the hard-class definition of the group. If a boy has his feet up we signal him ('four on the floor, thanks') with a non-verbal simulation of chairs legs—four fingers pointing down. 'But I can still hear you,' the student replies. 'I know you can, (partial agreement) but considerate manners in our room are feet and chair on the floor. Thanks.' I resumed the lesson; he slowly put his feet down with a loud sigh. If he hadn't I'd have cut my losses at that point (with a reminder of a deferred consequence) and carried on with the lesson. Effectively this avoids an unnecessary power struggle, puts the responsibility back where it belongs—to the student—minimises attention to the student, and keeps the focus on the main game with the assurance this will be followed up later.

Some teachers ignore what they should address and address (sometimes overdo) what they should tactically ignore. Getting a reasonable balance isn't easy. Discussion with colleagues on these issues will help, as will observing effective teachers in their own classrooms and focusing on how such colleagues utilise their corrective language and manner, and how they deal with behaviour issues. You could even sit in on their follow-up with students if they are comfortable about this. Peer mentoring (*elective* peer mentoring) is probably the most effective way of learning 'on the job'. This is further addressed in Chapter 9.

If we choose to ignore events that significantly affect our rights as teachers, we indicate acceptance. I was team teaching in a Year 8 class, and saw a student walk right in front of the teacher while she was making a point. Apparently she'd had it happen many times before! She had got used to it and accepted it, as had the class. It made her group attention almost impossible. If such behaviour has been frequent, over time, it may be a form of harassment (even bullying) and needs to be addressed at that level. No teacher should accept continual abuse of fundamental respect and fair treatment. The issue of teacher bullying is addressed in Chapter 9.

Closing the lesson

It is important to have a clear ending to the lesson that isn't rushed with work not collected, chairs still 'out', litter on floor, students beating the bell and so on:
- Give a signal for the end-of-lesson transition. Go to the positional place (at the front/centre or some familiar place where eyes and ears can be

seen en masse). This is sometimes called *anchoring*. Give a signal (the class bell, clapping, the tinkling of a glass or even the simple waiting for 10 seconds) and the direction 'stop (what you're doing), look (this way) and listen' *before* the directions about packing-up. If we speak over their on-task noise half the students may have already packed up but the other half may still be engaged in chatting, finishing work and so on. Some teachers give pack-up directions *while* still moving around the room, but it is more effective to go to the front/centre (p 63).

- Summarise the key aspects of the lesson where appropriate and where necessary. Review the key aspects of learning with the class if there is time.
- On Day One, pack up early enough to go through the routines for pack-up and exit from the classroom.
- Regarding homework reminders, a reminder sheet can help, or at least write the information on the chalkboard rather than a hurried verbal reminder. Many teachers use a homework book for all homework even if the homework is on a sheet. Some teachers give homework certificates for five days' completed homework and a 'reward' after five certificates.

Again, as with all routines, a check with colleagues will give insight into a range of options for creative homework. Some schools run homework clubs for students who would have little hope of completing homework at home because of family dysfunction or space problems. These clubs are run with the support of parents, and afternoon tea is provided to charge up the batteries and enhance the relaxed tone of homework club (two nights a week for 45 minutes).

- Clean-up routines need to be especially focused in areas such as art, textiles and manual arts. Posters on the wall or a few cartoons can help with the key steps in cleaning up the clay area, or around the lathe or sewing machine, for example. These posters should be located in the key areas: wet area, paint brushes area, clean-up/storage, tool areas, use of machines and so on. Again, it is catering for visual learners (words and pictures). At lower primary level a laminated card on each group's table can carry several clean-up reminders with little cartoons of what students need to do before the bell (and at the end of the day).
- It may be helpful to allocate room cleaning on a monitor system with monitors for key requirements/roles. The monitor system is rotated so all get the chance to do all jobs required.

- Little games like 'beat the clock' can help at lower primary level. 'OK, by the time I've counted backwards from 60 (or sung two verses of this song) I want to see a clean floor, chairs under tables, felt-tip pens with lids on in your containers . . .' Have the list on the wall or on their tables (with a little picture against each task).
- Have a final, calm settling time prior to the school-wide recess bell.
- Have a positive close to the lesson even if it's been a bad day or a bad class. Avoid saying, 'You're the worst class I've ever had! Do you hear? Yes you—you, Damian Scraggs—you're the worst!' If we've had a bad day, of course we need to acknowledge it—briefly: 'OK, it hasn't been the best lesson in the world. I'm especially concerned about . . . [here be specific and brief]. Tomorrow will be a new day. I'll expect better from you (and me) such as . . . Enjoy the rest of this day, folks. I'll see you tomorrow.' Of course, we'll keep back the one or two individuals for a brief after-class chat or make an appointment to discuss behaviour or learning concerns (p 84).
- If several students 'race off' when the bell goes, call them back. When they are settled, remind them that this is not a group detention but a group reminder. Class detentions are hated by students because they are unjust and do not achieve their peer-pressure objective. Then direct the students to leave again—considerately this time. The teacher stands by the door giving a goodbye to the now more-subdued members of the class as they leave. The teacher has established a small but important routine.
- Remind students to put chairs under the table (even at secondary level): 'Do the next class a favour, folks' or 'Do the cleaner a favour and pick up any litter near your table—everyone, two bits each. I'll give you a hand. You can drop it in the bin on the way out.'
- Lastly, remind students to leave the room in a way that considers others who are outside in the corridor: 'We walk (we don't run). We keep our voices at partner level. Thank you, see you tomorrow.' Some teachers will just let the students race off—literally—when the bell goes, to barge into yet another horde of 25 plus students across the corridor.

Encouraging the individual and the class

In a hard class there is often a tone of defeat—teachers are discouraged by what they face day after day. This can sometimes show up in their characteristic language. Teachers may actually be unaware that they are frequently using discouraging language: 'When will you ever learn?', 'What's wrong with you, eh?' or 'I'm sick and tired of your stupid behaviour'.

I recall working with a team of colleagues 'cracking' a couple of hard Year 8 classes. After a team-teaching session one colleague said, 'How is it possible to stay positive with that lot, especially that cretin Steven?' I understood his feelings—it isn't easy. We feel that they've let us down, that they do it on purpose, and that they don't deserve anything positive from us. One of the more common remarks I've heard from some teachers is why should we praise such and such—that's what they're supposed to be doing anyway!

Encouragement is the necessary balance to correction. It is the *conscious* effort to acknowledge and build up what is positive in the class or in the group.

I've seen teachers transform a class by consciously making the effort to acknowledge and affirm students' effort, publicly (where appropriate) and often in the quiet word aside from the main group.

Some of my colleagues jot down, in a notebook, students' extra little efforts or a contribution in their work or social interaction so they can quietly pass it on later, for example 'I like the way you handled that, Paul', 'That's a tidy desk there, Halid—looks well organised' or 'Look at the progress you've made in this . . . [be briefly specific] Lisa.'

When a student hands in minimal work, for example, it's tempting to comment only on poor work, just give a mark out of 10 or just fill the page with red (negative) marks. Acknowledge any effort the student has made: 'Well, Michelle, that's a positive line about Van Gogh's loneliness being the start of his madness. It helps the reader to understand. It will help if you go back and check the second point in the essay topic about how it affected his artwork. Check the underlined words for spelling and check for the date. I look forward to seeing your revised paper. Thanks. Mr Rogers.'

Encouragement is giving a bit of courage—through positive feedback—along the way to improve something. Sure, this approach takes a little longer until it becomes habit, but it develops a more positive and constructive tone in the learning environment.

Such encouragement acknowledges students' efforts and leaves the primary evaluation to them. What we convey is our confidence in their ability to progress. This can be done in the following ways:
• Describe the effort or thought you see in their behaviour, their work and their attitude: 'David, that's a tidy desk, mate', 'That's a clean work area—brushes all washed' (art), 'You've got your hand up'.
• Recognise the improvement made by the student.
• Reframe comments from the easily negative to the positive. For example, 'This is a noisy line' (said to a class lining up) and 'Don't you know what quiet means, eh?' becomes 'Settle down everyone, we've all lined up then?' The teacher comments on the students who have settled and gives them a 'good morning' (a smile) and makes a non-verbal hand gesture to the several noisy and physically restless students. 'Right, let's go in quietly and sit on the mat up the front.' Those few words preface expectation and are preventative management.

Encouragement creates the atmosphere conducive to positive learning: 'Look at the progress you've made' (specify), 'You've got a real talent for . . .' and 'I've got confidence in you because . . .' This challenges the student to look forward and to be specific about things that can change the present for the better: 'That helped a lot, Hung. It looks a lot tidier in the reading corner now. It'll be easier to find the books, eh?'

Encouragement works in the following ways:
• Acknowledge even the little that the students accomplish, and help them to focus on areas that they may need to work on or what still needs to be

done: 'It's very tidy over there. The lids are on the felt-tip pens. What's left to do?' The teacher points to the pencil shavings.

• Avoid disclaiming after encouraging, for example 'You've got your hand up, Michael.' (Teacher smiles.) 'If you had you're hand up all the time it would be so much better, wouldn't it, eh?' Also, avoid using encouragement in any way to manipulate the child.

• Some students will benefit from a personal plan for their class work or behaviour (p 108) as a way to motivate and encourage.

• A positive note (or phone call) home can be very rewarding for a student, especially when previous phone calls (or letters) have been of the 'We are disappointed with . . .' variety. Some primary schools use a good-news book between parent(s) and school to acknowledge the students' assets, special talents, contributions and so on.

• Observe and note social skills (primary). When a teacher observes a student displaying thoughtful social skills—in the playground for example—the duty teacher makes a note and passes it back to the grade teacher. It could be 'good winning', 'respecting others by . . .' or 'suggesting instead of bossing' (McGrath and Francey 1993).

• Classroom meetings (primary) can be used to give positive feedback to class members (peer feedback). When students give feedback in a classroom meeting setting, it is important that they acknowledge what it is they like or appreciate about their peer(s). For example, 'I appreciate Michael's help in maths because . . .' or 'Lisa is kind when she . . .'

• Keep it genuine—'fair dinkum'. When it's appropriate it's worth finishing the day (or session) with 'Thanks, everyone—I've really enjoyed being with you all today.' It is also important for the whole class, and especially for the hard class, for the teacher to make a conscious effort (BDN) to begin and end the day or session positively (p 13).

• If students don't always respond to our encouragement, keep it going anyway. We don't need to add qualifiers, such as 'I really mean it!' or 'Well, if that's the way you feel, I won't say anything nice.' Their unenthusiastic or even negative response ('I don't think my work's any good!') may be a form of attention seeking, or just habit. Maybe they haven't had much encouragement at home.

• Basically, it's treating people with respect—even if they don't 'deserve' it.

Motivation

Motivating a hard class is a challenge, especially in subject areas they don't enjoy. Motivation requires a reasonable balance between the intrinsic and extrinsic motivation at work in a group.

Intrinsic motivation involves:
* the need for 'challenges' in learning situations
* meeting fundamental needs such as the need to belong, the need for fun and the acknowledgment of worth
* the natural drives for interest and curiosity—this is where teachers utilise novelty, prior knowledge, selecting topics likely to interest the age/group
* likelihood of success—if students believe they're not going to be successful academically or their reputation is already 'shot', they've got nothing to lose; that is why it is important to cater for mixed abilities within the group through individual education plans and, where appropriate, peer mentoring, and it is also important to balance co-operative group learning with individual learning.

Extrinsic motivation involves:
* creating a context (through classroom environment, teaching method, content and the rights/rules establishment) that enhances the naturally intrinsic motivation, for example the classroom meetings approach (p 33), the group establishment approach (p 41) and the group reinforcement activities motivate students' needs to have a say, and to feel they are significant and can appropriately influence how things are
* the status of the subject or grades, or parent expectations (even sibling expectations)—these may be powerful extrinsic reinforcers for students for good or ill (for example, 'Why can't you be more like your brother?').

Children respond to a range of motivators and reinforcers:
* Many students appreciate a certificate when they know they've put in the hard graft in a cultural area, community service or school service, as well as in academic and sport areas (even here certificates can acknowledge effort and improvement as well as outcomes).
* I've come across several schools now that have what they call a 'gold card' (the size of a Bankcard). This laminated card carries the student's passport-sized photo with name, date of birth and signature. A gold-card holder is a student who is consistently cited as someone who is making the effort across a wide range of areas to be a contributing member of the school community. Gold-card holders are entitled to discounts on a range of local services and additional library borrowing. It is a way of acknowledging the larger group of students who 'consistently do the right thing' (as one school notes). It is an affirmation of a student's social effort, maturity and responsibility.
* As with all extrinsic motivation, it is important to be careful not to set up a situation where students behave well only

because there's a pay-off. Staff will need to discuss how they can best motivate individuals and indeed whole classes. By planning curriculum, lesson units and teaching methods in teams, we can share experiences and approaches we have found to be beneficial to motivate positive learning experiences.

- Teacher motivation can energise a class and pull it out of the spiral of bad feeling and lack of success. I've seen very challenging classes turn around within a term when teachers have:
  —planned together and worked as a team
  —moved away from easy blame and labelling
  —involved students in the re-establishment process (p 41)
  —provided challenging material
  —acknowledged and affirmed the effort of individuals and the group
  —not given up.

Classroom management

'Pupils are typically reported as liking teachers who can keep order (without being too strict), are fair (that is, are consistent and have no favourites), can explain clearly and give help, give interesting lessons, and are friendly and patient (Kyriacou 1986, p 139). Studies of classroom discipline indicate that much pupil misbehaviour actually stems from a sense that a teacher who is unable to fulfil such demands (that is, demands of the teaching and management role) is felt to be offensive by pupils and thereby provokes them into misbehaviour (ibid, pp 139–140).

I've had many classroom meetings with students where we've analysed, as a class, where they believe things are going wrong. The common refrain to much of their feedback is:

- 'You can do what you want in here and he won't check up.'
- 'I hate this subject and I hate how it's taught—I mean it's the same each time we come and there's no different things.' (I think the student meant 'no variability'.)
- 'Sometimes she'll yell at us and then she doesn't care what happens on other days!'

I've had students say, in effect, that in some classes they will engage in group 'payback'—that is, if this is how it's going to be we might as well get some satisfaction here. I've seen classes 'lay down tools' and refuse to do *this* subject with *this* teacher in *this* way.

These students are not just simply being difficult (there's always one or two ringleaders who will capitalise on any unfocused group energy). They are often reacting to what they perceive is unfair or poor treatment of them as a class.

If the teacher can acknowledge their discontent *early* and seek their co-operation, changes can occur. Of course, if the spiral of discontent and failure is allowed to become embedded into Term 2 or 3, it will be very much harder to really turn things around. In a supportive school environment colleagues will be alert to the hard-class signals and set up intervention and support processes.

Hallmarks of an effective teacher are as follows:

- Be at class on time (p 13).
- Check out the classroom environment beforehand if at all possible (seating, number of seats, chalkboard, flickering fluorescent lights, glare and so on). This is especially important when stuck in a demountable classroom.
- Have relevant materials, worksheets and even writing implements (p 67).
- Have work for those with significant learning problems, unless they are on individual learning programs or the teaching approach is based on group learning.
- Learn student names early and use their names often in all situations.
- Have the relevant 'toilet' or 'out-of-class' passes with you (know the routines for legitimate class exit).
- Teach the basic routines for entry, settling, on-task and exit in the first lesson (for example, cues for teacher assistance—p 66).
- Have the rules published in a positive way.
- Go over, with the students, their basic responsibilities. These correspond to the rules and cover fairness, good manners and basic respect. Specifically, over time, they will address such issues as positive language (no put-downs), care for equipment/property, consideration for personal space and work noise level (p 69).
- Make sure on Day One that little time is lost in finding seats and getting organised. Plan for this—it won't just happen.
- Have some simple whole-class instructions on Day One (beyond the basic rights/rules focus). This could be a learning focus that is both enjoyable and easy to accomplish—even some activities with familiarity (especially important at the elementary level).
- In time the normative routines for wet-day, circle-time (on the mat), quiet reading time, lunch and so on can be taught.
- It is helpful to quietly establish a positive managerial and disciplinary style—not bossy but confident. Monitoring of positive behaviours is important on Day One. Effective scanning and intervention, even on minor issues, can set the tone for subsequent class behaviours.

Chapter 6

FOLLOWING UP WITH DISRUPTIVE STUDENTS

Winning or losing points becomes a conflict in itself and not just a discussion about conflict. It is something of an absurdity to try to solve one conflict with another one.

Edward De Bono, Conflicts: A Better Way to Resolve Them

I finished the lesson. I reminded the students about leaving the room tidy ('I'll give you a hand', 'tidy tables', 'chairs under . . . ' and 'litter off the floor'). Just before the bell went I said, 'Goodbye for now'. I took my notebook from my top pocket and read out the names, 'I need to see Leigh and Darren for a few moments after class.' Darren groaned and Leigh pushed back his chair and swore loudly under his breath, grunted, and then scowled and sulked. 'What'd I do anyway?' he asked. I wasn't about to start any discussion. Leigh and Darren had been play punching earlier in the lesson— the final straw being the pen jabbing in the last five minutes of English.

I said, 'I can see you're uptight, Leigh, I won't keep you long.' I farewelled the class, and Leigh and Darren stayed back. Leigh stood against the wall near the door, sulking. I spoke briefly with the boys, separately, and covered the following:

- I acknowledged how they might be feeling (they'd be missing some recess).
- I focused on the behaviour and how it had affected basic rights (especially learning).
- I invited some feedback.
- I 'mirrored' (p 88) their behaviour and they laughed when I briefly mirrored their so-called 'play fighting'.
- I invited their feedback again and we finally made a brief verbal plan about where they would sit next lesson.
- I wrote down their suggestion, determined to hold them to it next lesson.
- We separated amicably.

In the establishment phase of the year it is important to follow up classroom incidents that, in the heat of the moment, indicate a need to follow up and follow through beyond the classroom correction.

Sometimes the follow-up will merely be an after-class chat to clarify an issue of concern. At other times it will be a consequence (cleaning up a mess, filling in a 4W Form—p 89). When pushed for time an appointment will need to be made with the student to follow up beyond the classroom. If the situation is particularly disturbing it may be helpful for the initiating teacher to invite a colleague to facilitate and support the follow-up.

Guidelines for follow-up

To help with consistency of practice concerning follow-up it is important to give consideration to fundamental, preferred practices:

1 Consider, as a staff, why follow-up is important in the first place, and what we are seeking to convey to students and (by proxy) to their peers. Fundamentally, we need to convey certainty of outcome, not intentional severity of outcome. With harder classes the follow-up can weed out the merely challenging from the very difficult. It can reduce an early domino effect. By following up with students early (even on Day One) we show that:

   • we care
   • we are concerned about their behaviour, their welfare and their learning
   • we want to give them some assistance (not a long lecture though)
   • we genuinely appreciate their side of the story where appropriate (4W Form) and we do take their feedback seriously
   • we expect them to work with us not against us.

   It is important that we convey concern and offer support. Follow-up is not an opportunity to 'win' at the expense of their losing. Some teachers use follow-up time to hammer home emotional payback ('How dare you think you can speak to me the way you did!' and so on).

2 Follow up on important, not trivial, issues. It is worth discussing with colleagues the sorts of issues that would normally merit an after-class chat or a follow-through consequence, such as cleaning up that wasn't done (or that the student refused to do) in class time, and whether we should keep students back to complete work. If we keep students back on trifling issues we will unnecessarily strain the relationship with them. For example, if, during class time, a student responds to a reminder, direction or question about behaviour in a very sarcastic, sulky or hostile manner, it will be worth following up to briefly focus on the tone and manner adopted (see later).

3 Briefly acknowledge how the student might be feeling. Tune in:
   • 'You look annoyed, Jason.'

- 'I can see you're annoyed, but I need to speak to you about . . . '
- 'It can be a hassle to have to miss a bit of recess, but I won't keep you long. I need to speak to you about . . . '

Many students are naturally annoyed at having to stay back after class (they are missing recess, and they also don't know what to expect from a teacher's follow-up, especially on Day One). It may help to follow with a question: 'Do you know why I've asked you to stay back?' (Few students will say, 'Yes I do, actually. I was being significantly disrespectful to you in class when I . . . ') But at least the question invites a bit of thought. I often add, where relevant, '*You're not in trouble*, Jason. I just need you to explain . . . ' and so on.

4 Focus on the *behaviour*—the specific behaviour that occurred in the classroom when they were calling out, butting-in, wandering, avoiding a task, being 'rude' in tone and manner, and so on. It may help to briefly 'mirror' the students' behaviour back to them, that is, re-create what it 'looked like' when they performed the offending behaviour (p 88).

5 Invite their feedback on what you have said or 'mirrored':
- 'Maybe you're having a bad day, Lisa?' (After all, students have bad days like us.)
- 'Can you think of what you can do differently if you're having a bad day in the future? How could you let me know without shouting and . . . ?'

Leave it at this point. Making your feelings known, raising awareness *and* acknowledging your joint humanity may well be enough for some students. Other students will give feedback that gives insight into their behaviour, their learning or some idiosyncratic need. This can alert us to garner wider support from the school counsellor, home-school liaison officer or some other source. Keep the focus on the behaviour all the time. Avoid getting sidetracked into what other students did or said, or what other teachers allow them to do, or that they don't like this subject. Acknowledge their comments and refocus back to the main issue: 'OK Leigh, it sounds as though you believe Damien does a heap of calling out too. I'll be speaking to him as well. For the moment . . . '

6 There are a number of basic relational skills to remember in all one-to-one settings, however brief the amount of time spent:
- Keep the classroom door open for ethical probity. With an extended one-to-one session with male teacher and female student, it is important to have a female colleague 'sitting in' nearby, doing something else.
- Calm yourself before trying to calm the student. Don't use loud voice tones or sarcasm, and keep the tone pleasant and invitational. Where it is appropriate, be firm without an aggressive tone of voice, stance or body language.
- Give the student psychological and personal space. Don't crowd the student or jab with a finger in the air to make a point. I've seen teachers jabbing students in the shoulder to make a point loudly in the corridor, so half the school hears.
- Avoid rushing the dialogue.
- Keep the focus on the primary issues that occurred, refer to the rule or right, and avoid arguing, for example:

Student: 'Yeah, well I don't do that all the time, do I?'
Teacher: 'I don't know. This is the first time I've had you in my class, Dean (partial acknowledgment/agreement). I do know your tone of voice was hostile when I . . .' (Be specific and brief about the hostility. The teacher then refers to the right regarding respect.)
Teacher: 'We've got a right in our classroom to respect. I don't speak to you like that and I don't expect you to speak like that to me. If you're uptight about something in class, even with me, and if you think I've been unfair [or whatever] then come and see me after class. Let me know so I can do something about it.' What is crucial is that our tone and manner is not hostile, mean-spirited or dominating. Our tone and manner will powerfully affect what we say and what is really heard.

7 Finish the after-class chat or after-class consequence with a *brief* reminder of what you expect next time in class and separate amicably: 'I appreciate you staying back, Damien. I just wanted to make sure you were aware of . . . We've got to live together for a whole year in 7C.' Here the teacher may smile and say, 'Catch you later' (and the student may give a wry grin back). It is really important not to hold grudges with students. Most students want to know that their teachers basically like them, that they are fair, and that they won't play favourites or have a 'downer' on them for the next day, week or term.

8 It is important to 'track' these students beyond the few after-class chats to see if their behaviour is more than 'BDS'. If there is some pattern to the behaviour we will need to look at a more whole-school approach to the follow-up (p 105).

Mirroring behaviour

One-to-one with a student is a way of briefly re-creating the emotional and behavioural moment (Rogers 1995). It re-creates what it looks like *when* students call out, butt in, push in line and so on. (I have actually mirrored floor rolling to five- and six-year-olds.) Note the following points:

- Only mirror a student's behaviour if it is within your comfort zone. If you're not comfortable with mirroring back to a student their tone of voice and behaviours such as calling out, butting-in, seat wandering or pushing in line, it may be better to just use action phrases and descriptive phrases: 'Nazim, when you had your feet up in class—you know, on the desk and leaning back—can you remember what you said and how you said it?' Here the teacher repeats the words instead of mirroring the sarcastic and insouciant tone of voice used by the student. The teacher describes how the voice sounded, 'It sounded really sarcastic, Nazim—as though you couldn't have cared less about having your feet up and also as though you didn't care about me either.'

- Ask the student's permission. If the student says 'no', just describe accurately. It may help to have a drawing or cartoon that can pictorially image the student's behaviour (Rogers 1994). When describing the behaviour it is important to show concern and support. Our confident follow-up is saying I'm concerned and I'm serious, but I'm inviting your understanding and your responsibility.

- Mirroring is illustrative only. Keep it brief. Never use it to embarrass students or to make students feel bad about themselves.
- After you have mirrored the behaviour, step back physically and become the calm (and caring) adult again. Point to the now vacated emotional space and say, '*That's* what it looks like, Craig, when you . . .' Some students may genuinely not know what their behaviour looks like, and how 'rude' or 'sarcastic' their tone of voice characteristically sounds. A lot of students will involuntarily laugh at their 're-created behaviour' (either from anxiety or because it does actually look daggy, even 'stupid', in retrospect). Acknowledge, 'Yes, it does look a bit funny, but in class, Craig, it's really annoying because . . .'

One of my colleagues mirrored back to a rather challenging Year 9 girl how she often entered the classroom. Apparently the normal after-class chats had not been 'taken up' by this student and so my colleague, in the *one-to-one* setting, 'became' Lisa for 30 seconds. Mirroring Lisa's typical behaviour, the teacher entered the room with a flamboyant notice-me look as he scanned the imaginary 20 pair of eyes alighting on her as she came in late—again. This teacher was a dab hand at drama. He imitated the way Lisa gave a 'snort' and said, 'What are we doing today then?', and the final sitting down with an extravagant leg-cross. This seemed to do the trick! 'Gees,' said Lisa, 'I don't cross my legs like *that*!' The teacher replied, 'You do, Lisa, well, pretty close to that.' The teacher pointed back to the now vacated 'kinaesthetic space'. The word *that* (as used by Lisa) now had meaning and specificity. Lisa gave an I-know-you-know grin and from here they had a productive chat about attention (p 115) and made a plan for a better way to enter the room.

The 4W Form

Rather than have a student writing lines as a punishment or consequence it can be more constructive to direct students to write about their behaviour. This approach is appropriate for those behaviour disruptions that are not serious but have a degree of frequency that is annoying. The 4W Form (Appendix 2) can be useful as a basic right of reply:

1 What I did against our class or school rules.
2 What rules (or rights) I broke or infringed.
3 What is my explanation?
4 What I think I should do to fix things up or work things out.
Have a place for the student and teacher to sign.

The value of the 4W approach is:
- It gives the student a right to reply.
- It provides the student with a chance to think through what happened.
- It refocuses the student's attention back to the right or rule affected by their behaviour.
- It gives a basis for further teacher–student (or even student–teacher) dialogue.
- Most of all, it concentrates on what the restitutional outcome ought to be (what I think I should do, or can do, to fix things up).
It is not helpful to force students to write, or to ask them to do it when they

are really uptight. After some cool-off time, the 'form' can be used to help students clarify things and refocus on what happened.

If the answers to the question on the form are basic ('I was bad' or 'I was naughty') help the student to extend or refocus. For example, say, 'In what way were you naughty? What did you do that was against our rules?' Students who really struggle with writing should not be forced or embarrassed by having to write out a reasonable response. We can instead ask the questions and reword their answers: 'So, is that what you mean?' or 'Are you saying that . . . ?' Small children can draw the four responses and the teacher can dialogue within that framework. The 4W Form is also a record of the students' attempt to come to terms with their behaviour. If there is no significant change using such an approach, an individual behaviour plan might be an appropriate next step.

Managing a crisis situation: Time-out

In hard classes there are often students who are catalysts for significant group inattention and disturbance: tantrums, running around the room, persistent refusal to respond to reasonable teacher requests, and so on. Most teachers in challenging schools can recount examples of students standing on desks shouting, 'You can't do nothing to me!' or the back-to-back disruptive pattern that just goes on and on and on with the persistent attention seeker or powerbroker desperate for an audience or a contest of wills.

No teacher should be left in the invidious position of having a student hold a class to ransom. Such behaviour not only stresses the teacher but also affirms, even confirms, that pattern of behaviour if it is allowed to continue ('I can do what I like and say what I like').

Time-out practices

Students learn in many ways but one of the more powerful ways is by association. If time-out is consistently associated with repeatedly disruptive or any dangerous behaviour then they will at least learn the following:
- Certain behaviours will never be tolerated.
- Refusal to respond to fair guidelines and fair discipline will result in temporary exclusion (time-out).
- As night follows day, time-out *will* happen here *when* you behave in unacceptable ways.
- All time-out occurs within the concept of 'choice' and of known, fair rules.
- The class is protected from extremes of behaviour, and time-out is seen as a just, short-term solution. The rights of the non-disruptive students are protected; this psychological protection gives the other students an assurance that something is being done for their benefit as well as the disruptive student.
- The disruptive student always has a chance to work on a personal behaviour change plan (p 104).

Time-out is probably the most intrusive short-term consequence a school will employ for disruptive behaviour. Time-out can occur in the classroom as a formal, even semiformal, cool-off time or it can involve temporary exclusion from the classroom. It is often used as a formal discipline mechanism across the school to temporarily exclude students from the classroom where their behaviour is significantly affecting fundamental safety, treatment and learning. Students should be supervised during time-out especially at primary level.

It is essential, especially in hard classes, that teachers have the assurance they are backed up by colleagues and administration in crisis situations. This is especially so where students refuse to leave a class. It's very distressing to see a teacher screaming at a recalcitrant student, 'Get out! Get out now!', and the student standing there laughing and saying, effectively (or really), 'You can't make me!' No matter how ineffective a teacher's management may be, no teacher deserves that.

The practical question is how do we get such students out of the room in a heated situation? Further, it may be more effective in the longer term to direct the student to leave (or arrange for the student to leave) before serious verbal conflict ensues! How can we do this on a whole-school basis?

In the first place, it is important that all teachers have a general consequential plan that is part of their establishment phase (rights/rules/responsibility/consequences—see p 49). For example, if a student makes it difficult for other students to learn or feel safe, one of the following will happen:
- Students will be reminded of the class rule.
- Students may be directed to work somewhere else in the room (relocation).
- Students may be directed to take cool-off time (COT). Some primary schools use the term 'take-five'. The students take five minutes COT away from others in another area of the room watching a five-minute egg timer (Rogers 1994).
- Students will be asked to stay back and discuss their behaviour with their teacher, fix things up or put things right (restitution).
- Students may be asked to leave the room or may be escorted from the room to a COT area—a time-out area or room. William Glasser (1991, pp 144, 145) describes a time-out room as a place in the school (a room):

> run by someone who has experience dealing with students who have
> been asked to leave class . . . The student may protest that it is unfair
> and that you are punishing him by keeping him there, but you have to point
> out that it is his choice not to begin to work on the solutions. As soon as he
> starts working on a solution, he can go back to class . . . he is always treated
> with courtesy . . . and offered counselling. He should be constantly reminded
> that no-one wants him to stay in restriction: Everyone wants him to begin
> work on the problem and will help in any way possible.

In addition, teachers need the security of a school-wide time-out plan for crisis situations. There should be a known, published procedure and plan to enable a teacher to direct very disruptive students from the classroom to a safe, supervised place where they can calm down, refocus and make some plan to re-enter the classroom in a way that considers others' rights. Some students will leave the classroom if directed aside and spoken to calmly and firmly: 'David, it's not working. I've asked you several times to settle down and . . . [be briefly specific about the behaviour and effect on you and others in the room]. It's better that you leave now. I'll get together with you later to see how we can work things out.'

Of course this implies the following:
- There is a place (and person) to which you can direct the student.
- The student will go.
- You will keep to your word and follow up with the student.
- If the student refuses to leave there is a back-up plan, for example a colleague *cue* system (see below).

As Glasser (1991) points out, 'All the students, including the one who has disrupted, should hear the message that "lead-managers" do not threaten. They recognise that there are problems and they try to solve them by themselves. They need the co-operation of the student.' (Glasser contrasts teachers who 'boss' by threats and coercion and teachers who manage by leading.) And, of course, if the student is unwilling to co-operate, assuming the teacher's approach is positive, then the student will need to be directed to leave the room.

If the student refuses to leave (at any age) there will need to be a simple, workable, back-up plan. This is essential. Many schools use a simple colleague *cue* system. Each teacher in the team or the faculty has small laminated cards containing their room number (coloured, say, green for 'go', or red for 'danger' even pink for 'calm'). In one primary school, for example, the standard printed card reads:

TIME-OUT: Could you please assist me as soon as possible in Room 17. Thank you.

_____

(Teacher's name)

This card can be sent with a trusted student to a colleague (generally a senior colleague) who will come as quickly as possible to that room and escort the disruptive student to a cool-off time area. Disruptive students will almost always go with a third party (another adult) simply because that teacher is not part of the conflict cycle in that room. If they refuse to leave the room with the senior teacher, it is more effective if the third-party teacher stays in the room while the class teacher escorts the rest of the class out of the room, away, to another area. When the audience has gone, the supporting third party can then escort the student to the time-out area. This is in preference to trying to drag out a kicking, yelling student who has a huge audience to 'feed on', especially at upper primary and secondary levels. Schools sometimes refer to this area as the 'time-out-room', 'work-it-out-room' or 'thinking area'. It is often at (or near) the administration section where students can be supervised while they settle down.

In the time-out area several posters with illustrations can adorn the wall opposite the seat and desk where the student sits. A poster could contain the following:

1 Think about why you have been asked to leave your classroom.
  ASK YOURSELF:
2 What did I do?
3 What is my side of the story ?
4 What rule did I break?
  5 What can I do to fix things up?

It is also helpful to have a poster on the wall with the school's rights and responsibilities for older students.

It is important that back-up time-out plans are well thought out and published as an in-house document. It is especially important that relief (supply) teachers and teachers new to school are taken through the policy and assured that use of time-out by a teacher is not a sign of weakness, but the way we do things in our school. It will be important to explain in a policy document to parents what is meant (philosophically) by time-out, why and how the school uses it, and most of all that it is a short-term consequence. Countless teachers have shared how such a simple, school-wide support procedure has given them confidence in their behaviour planning and reduced their stress levels at school.

Caveat Some teachers will initially use (or overuse) the time-out card system for minor disruptive behaviours. It is important to do the following:
- Explain the appropriate use of the time-out card: safety, back-to-back disruptions, perception of a possible crisis, and persistent refusal to obey a reasonable teacher request are the sorts of situations requiring the use of time-out support. However, behaviour such as a student merely sulking or avoiding a task can be tactically ignored and followed up later, providing it's not really affecting others.
- Make sure that records are kept by the initiating teacher and the administration (in part to see which teachers may be having problems with difficult students). These records will be needed for parent notification, case conferences and simple tracking of the student to see if any future correction, mediation and behaviour plans are having any effect on behaviour.
- Make sure that the initiating teacher is involved in follow-up *beyond* time-out itself. This is especially important at secondary level where some teachers feel that if a student is sent to time-out the problem is finished as far as they are concerned. (The expectation is that the year-level-co-ordinator will send back the recalcitrant 'fixed'.)

Think about why you have been asked to leave the classroom.

- Time-out rarely changes behaviour in the longer term. It is a short-term solution to give support to the teacher, the rest of the class and the disruptive student. It is essential that a student be supported with an individual behaviour management plan if they have been in time-out several times for similar patterns of behaviour (p 104).

One primary school lists its time-out policy this way:

Time-out
Time-out is used in the classroom or playground to help people cool down and think about what they have done wrong. Time-out only happens after someone has been reminded about a rule they have broken.*

If you are given time-out in the classroom, you go and sit on your own for a few minutes to sort out how you are going to put things right. This may be in the classroom or in another room.

If you are given time-out in the playground, you go and sit (away from others) on a seat for a few minutes to think about how you can make things right.

Hare Street Primary School, Harlow, UK

* This means, of course, reminded a few times, not just once. It implies a pattern of behaviour and refusal to respond to fair reminders of the rule.

Staff survey: Exit/Time-out policy review

1 How often do you (as a class/subject teacher) use exit/time-out (that is, directing a student away from your classroom to a colleague's class, administration or the time-out room)? Distinguish between usage of in-class and out-of-class time-out.
2 What sort of behaviour or situations do you use exit/time-out for?
3 How often do you use exit/time-out? (Once a day/several times a week/weekly/a few times a term)
4 How do you follow up your exit/time-out?
5 What is the school (or faculty) policy for:
   - use of time-out in the immediate short term?
   - following-up of behaviours that initiated the time-out episodes? (Time-out is a 'primary' consequence often needing 'secondary' consequences to follow through.)
   - students who refuse to leave the classroom for time-out?
   - students who have been in time-out several times (in close succession) for similar behaviours (and across several class settings)?

Classroom rotation

One of the variations of time-out (largely used at primary level) is *classroom rotation*. The student is enrolled in another class for at least one period a week to give the grade teacher a formal break from the behaviourally disordered student. These students tend to *never* have a day off, they tend not to be school refusers and some parents will personally admit they cannot stand to have them at home.

The student takes set work from their host class and does that work in another setting. It will need to be explained to the student and their parent(s) that this is not punishment. It is part of the support program for the student and the grade teacher.

Follow-up and three-way facilitation

Some follow-up may need to include a face-to-face meeting between a protagonist or perpetrator and a 'victim'. In hard classes, because of the regularity of silly (and hurtful) comments being made, some teachers do not follow up or follow through. 'It's not worth it,' some say, 'I'd be keeping back several kids each session.' It *is* worth the effort of follow-up in the establishment phase because it says you know, you care and you will not tolerate abusive, racist, put-down behaviour, graffiti on desks and so on. In this case a three-way approach (class teacher, support teacher and students in conflict with each other) may be helpful, where each side recounts their version of who pushed who off the chair or whatever happened (p 38). It can also help to run a classroom meeting specifically addressing classroom language and respect (p 37).

In most cases it is desirable for the grade/subject teachers to do their own follow-up or follow-through as this enhances teachers' appropriate role/leadership with the students as well as demonstrating care and support. In some settings with very challenging students, however, the follow-up will need mediation or, at the very least, facilitation.

- Have a school-wide due process for supported follow-up. This school-wide process needs to be there for issues of concern that a teacher feels cannot be solved by teacher–student dialogue alone, or for those situations where teachers do not feel confident in pursuing a one-to-one dialogue on their own. If a male teacher wants to pursue an extended one-to-one meeting with a female student, ethical probity and commonsense would see the need for a female facilitator. Staff need to be assured that there will always be facilitation support for conflict resolution and mediation, that there is a school-wide due process, that there is no shame in seeking colleague assistance in resolving difficult issues with students, and that the initiating of a three-way facilitation is part of the process (as distinguished from simple, quick 'buck passing').

- Make sure that it is genuinely 'three way', that is, the initiating teacher, the student (or students) and the support colleague who facilitates and/or mediates all have an appropriate 'say'. Part of the problem of facilitation is that some teachers are not able to accept that the student has a right of 'equal voice' in conflict mediation and resolution. This needs to be clarified in the school-wide due process. Some teachers persist in butting in while the student is giving their version (or perception) of events, and some even refuse to talk. That is why another teacher being present can assist in mediation.

- Make sure, too, there has been ample cool-off time between the disruptive event(s) and the three-way facilitation.

- It can be helpful to take notes at the meeting (it says 'we take this issue very seriously'). The facilitation role is to make sure that teacher and student(s) have a voice. The facilitation will clarify the issues and the comments, keep the parties on track and work for an appropriate resolution. The 4W questions can be useful as a guide at this meeting (p89).

If the student is *repeatedly* disruptive a recommendation for an individual management plan may well be a useful outcome of the three-way process.

At all times the focus is how the issue at stake affects the basic rights and responsibilities of teacher, student and the class as a whole.

Students who refuse to stay back after class

Some students will race off at the end of a class session even though the teacher has specifically directed them to stay back (this is more common at secondary level than primary). The teacher may barely get the last words in: 'If you choose not to stay back, I'll have to follow it up at . . . ' The student mutters, while walking or running off, 'Yeah, well, it's recess. Anyway, I didn't do anything! I'm not staying back!' It doesn't take the student long to reach the exit door and perceived freedom. It is probably a power struggle being played out here. It will be unhelpful (though tempting) to chase the miscreant down the corridor into the playground.

If a student doesn't stay back or keep an appointment (to discuss his behaviour or follow through with consequences), it is still important to follow up. It is important to communicate the *certainty* of the follow-up, even if it is several days later (as it may well have to be at secondary level).

I have at times used my off-class time to follow up students in other class settings. Sometimes it's just enough to have a brief chat in the corridor. I've knocked on a colleague's door and asked to see a student and noticed the student's eyes look back, not believing I'd actually follow up several days later. I've never had a colleague refuse me the option of 'withdrawing' a student from class for a brief chat, outside or in the interview room near the office. I always carry a notebook (p 85) to remind me of whom to track, and a brief note to remind me of the issue. It is easy to 'forget' in a busy week.

Apologies

It was the task avoidance that annoyed the teacher. He'd gone back to Peter at least half a dozen times: 'C'mon, get working, Peter. The bell's going soon!' Peter snapped back, 'Yeah, well you're picking on me!' The teacher replied, 'Don't you speak to me like that! How dare you! I'll have you on a detention!' As the teacher walked off, Peter mumbled, 'Gees you're an a . . . hole!' To which the teacher said, 'Right! Get out, go on, get out! Go to the principal now!' No doubt the teacher was fed up with the boy's intransigence—he was angry. He'd taken it personally.

The principal had a chat with Peter and with the teacher (after he'd cooled down). The principal managed to encourage Peter to agree to apologise for what he'd said. They went to the teacher together and the student, frowning, looked at his teacher (whose arms were folded) and said, 'Sorry I swore and that.' The teacher looked at him and said, 'No, I'm not having that! You don't mean it.' Here is an adult (nearly 40 years old) speaking to a 12-year-old with an unfair expectation, not even acknowledging the student's effort. Imagine what might have happened if the teacher had said, 'Well, Peter, it's not easy to apologise, but you made the effort. I guess we were both angry, eh? If you get uptight again, can you say it in a more helpful way?' Here the teacher wryly smiles and extends his hand.

Some teachers find it very difficult, even demeaning, to apologise *to* a student or work through a reconciliation. It is as if the teacher is somehow condescending to the minor, and is conveying weakness instead of modelling reconciliation. If we apologise or pursue reconciliation when it is appropriate, students are often very forgiving. It comes back to respect.

If we've got unnecessarily angry with a class or gone 'over the top' (we know when we've done it), an apology will clear the air. It doesn't have to be sycophantic, just genuine. Describe what you have done or said, and why you believe it happened that way. Keep it brief. Leave it, then, to their goodwill.

Detentions

The most easily wielded and overused punishment in schools is detention, especially at secondary level. Detentions, though, can be an easy way out for the class teacher in that the problem is referred to someone else to detain and punish the students. I've been in many schools where students from various classes sit waiting against the clock or just doing homework, while the teacher who initiated the detention engages in no actual conflict resolution. It has also been my experience that overuse of detentions in hard classes is self-defeating in the long term. The least effective detentions are class-based—keeping back the whole class for the misdemeanours of the several. Whole-class detentions are used by some teachers to punish the hard class. Distinguish between a whole-class after-class chat and a whole-class detention (p 78).

If detentions are going to be effective in any way there needs to be a school-wide, team-based or faculty-based framework for their use. Further, if the detention is seen as a *consequence* and not merely as a referral punishment (passing the problem student along the line) it can be used to teach students something positive. There are, of course, times when the behaviour of students is so severe that referral needs to be immediate and to senior staff.

In a survey, 'Attitudes of British secondary school teachers and pupils to rewards and punishments', Caffyn (1989) notes, 'In [this] present study the giving of detentions was rated as significantly more effective both by teachers and pupils in the school which gave them rarely and operated a well-run system. Obtain the optimum balance between "good use" and "overuse".'

It is the association in the student's minds between sparingly used and frequently used that gives detention any useful 'currency'. If teachers are giving detentions for every kind of misdemeanour from not having equipment and lateness through to verbal abuse the currency is 'devalued'.

Detention needs to be seen within a wider framework of consequences and punishment:
- after-class chats—not really a punishment at all, more a clarification of what behaviours are affecting mutual rights and working on student understanding and restitution where necessary
- catch-up time where a student completes or continues some piece of set work

- clean-up (mess the student had left earlier in the lesson)
- the 4W Form (p 89)
- detention as (a *formal* process of detaining the student with notification to parent, a set time and a due process geared to working on the behaviour and not just 'doing time'
- year co-ordinator/teacher behaviour contract
- accountability conference (p 150)
- suspension, parent conference and so on.

In other words a school needs a consequential framework that has degrees of seriousness relative to how behaviour affects fundamental rights and how significantly and repetitively it affects those rights.

Key questions to be answered in developing and using a detention policy are:

- What is the point of detaining a student? To inconvenience, punish or create some psychological payback?
  - Assuming we follow the Education Department guidelines for detention, what are we trying to achieve in a set stay-back or stay-in time?

Although these are obvious questions for consideration and policy planning, detention can be so entrenched in usage in a school that serious whole-school reflection may not have been given to this topic. We need to know answers to the following:

- What do we want the student to learn (if anything) from detention?
- Do we want the students to just sit there or work on a 4W-type feedback (p 89)? Work on a behaviour plan? Plan any accountability or restitution? Do set work? Do any work quietly? Have a litter duty (some sort of civic accountability)?
- What sort of behaviours do we agree would 'merit' detention?
- Should detention be faculty based or year-level based? Is there a place for subject-teacher detention?
- If detention is conducted by a teacher other than the referring teacher, what is the responsibility of both teachers in detaining the student? It is easy for a subject or class teacher to refer the student to someone else and just leave it at that—no further responsibility and no effective resolution.
- What written outcomes can be used to track and process detention? Do several detentions in succession equal some sort of referral for an individual behaviour plan? How does that work at our school?

It is worth publishing the detention policy and framework/philosophy of use, especially for beginning teachers and those new to the school.

Suspension and expulsion

Suspension is a serious 'step' in a consequential chain. However, it needs to be part of a school's behaviour-management policy because:
- it gives a formal cooling-off time for the student
- it indicates to the rest of the class and school that the behaviour resulting in suspension is serious and will not be tolerated.

Suspension can be in-school suspension or at-home suspension. When it occurs in school, suspension is an extension of the time-out room concept. Work is set, no extra school privileges are allowed and recess times are taken separately from other students.

Suspension has to be backed up by careful follow-through, and geared to problem solving and restitution processes with the key participants and stakeholders. Any student who has faced a few suspensions would normally go on to an individually supervised plan and contract supervision (Chapter 8). Obviously suspension is not a consequence to be used lightly. It is properly used for severe misbehaviours rather than the last straw in a chain of less serious behaviours that are best dealt with by effective follow-up procedures.

Suspension should also be attended by appropriate 'ceremonial formality' (Positive Discipline, note 7, 1989):
- An appearance before senior staff and reporting teacher(s), and even a 'suspension committee'. Suspensions are not conducted merely at the whim of an individual teacher. It can help if the school behaviour policy outlines the sorts of behaviours that occasion suspension.
- Focus on the certainty and justice of the act of suspension.
- Offer whatever support is possible to parents while emphasising student responsibility.
- Offer to the students the support of an individual behaviour management plan (p 104).

Expulsion is a very serious step, even a traumatic step, for a school to take. However, a student (and sometimes their family) cannot be allowed to continue to disrupt the safety and welfare of a school. In some cases the student (through persistent harassment and bullying) may well be effectively holding a school to ransom. This cannot be allowed to continue. If a student (and their family) has continued to flout the school's reasonable code of behaviour, and refused to work with supportive measures such as counselling and behaviour plans, a school needs to consider the safety and learning rights of the rest of the students and act accordingly.

Normally a school will pursue alternative options, rather than *formal* expulsion. Such processes would have been developed over a number of case conferences with parents and school, and with Education Department personnel.

One of the problems for schools in the current economic environment is that there are very few options outside formal schooling for recidivist students. Notwithstanding that hard reality, expulsion still needs to be an option for schools.

Chapter 7

PATTERNS OF BEHAVIOUR AND CHANGING BEHAVIOUR

The young people of today think of nothing but themselves. They have no reverence for parents or old people. They talk as if they alone know everything and what passes for wisdom with us is foolishness to them.

Peter the Hermit (1098)
(cited in Conway 1974)

First principles of behaviour management

Behaviour, that is, human behaviour, is a complex phenomenon. There is no single, simple reason for people to act supportively, co-operatively, thoughtfully, carelessly, meanly, nastily and aggressively. The first principles of behaviour management are as follows:

1 Behaviour is *learned*. Children learn by association (both good and bad) what behaviours receive approval and/or disapproval. They also learn from the modelling of significant others. Of course, if unhelpful, poor and ineffective behaviour is learned, it can be unlearned and relearned. This is the power of new association, new modelling and the development of new behaviour skills.

2 Behaviour is *conditioned*. Conditioning is another form of learning, largely from one's environment and not always reflective (especially in younger children). If a home environment is dysfunctional with emotional abuse, frequent yelling, put-downs, harsh nagging and frequent physical discipline, it will have an effect on behaviour. Bullying, as one example, has its early 'learning' from conditioning at home—that first social laboratory where words, gestures, emotions and beliefs are tracked into often unreflective and habitual behaviours. At school teachers pick up the residue of that conditioning. The home environment is outside our significant control. Of course, we will report to relevant authorities if we believe the child is at risk but we can't, from school, change the dysfunctional home environment. This should not deter us, however, from realising the powerful effect schools can have on students from disadvantaged and dysfunctional home environments. School curriculum, teaching style and method, learning styles, consideration of prior content knowledge of our students, working with the natural desire to learn, grouping of students, school welfare programs, catering for a range of educational and social options to enhance access and success through school, encouragement and even the classroom environment can all significantly affect learning and social outcomes at school. (Rutter et al 1979; Rogers 1995).

3 Behaviour is *purposeful* in a social setting. Children are not *just* naughty (at least not all the time). Dreikurs et al (1982) note that mistaken social goals of attention and power see students engage in disturbing classroom behaviour that enables (in the child's private logic) a sense of social

belonging. All children (all people) have a fundamental need to belong in social settings. If children don't believe they can belong in socially reasonable, acceptable ways, they 'learn' to belong by persistent calling out, rolling on the mat, butting in and so on. These types of behaviour that teachers regularly see in students are often the students' way of saying 'Notice me' or 'This is how I confirm I belong.' If attention seeking (a natural need) is overserviced early and often, children will believe that this is how they can 'belong'. The exercise of seeking attention, power or revenge in a setting such as school has to be seen in its social context in the public domain of classroom, corridor or playground. Here students have an audience that (in their private logic) they believe is acknowledging, affirming or supporting their attention-seeking or power-provoking behaviours. In the hard-class setting some students make a career out of exercising these 'behavioural goals'. It is a challenge to work with these students to help them identify what their behavioural/social 'goal' is, to acknowledge why they are doing it, and to support them in a process of behaviour change without denying the need for appropriate consequences. This is further developed in the section on 'goal disclosure' (p 115).

4   Behaviour is *chosen*. It is unhelpful to treat students as if they are merely the victims of an emotional or causative pathology over which they have no control. When a student spits at another, swears abusively, kicks a chair over and so on, there is an element of choice. Of course, that choice is conditioned by the past and by the context; it may well be affected by a behaviour disorder such as attention-deficit disorder (ADD). But ADD doesn't cause aggressive anti-social behaviour—it contributes to it. Once you say students just can't help their behaviour, you do them and their families a disservice. Far better to *teach* students how to make better choices, and then hold them responsible and accountable for the choices they then make and the consequences that go with those choices.

5   Behaviour *communicates information about needs*. It is hard (not impossible, but hard) to behave thoughtfully and considerately. It is hard for a student to learn well at school if their school day carries significant inner turmoil from home. All of us have bad days and some students' bad days are constant. If their teachers are not considerate of their welfare and basic needs and do not 'read' the students' behaviour then the classroom can be a place of continued conflict. It is possible to be both considerate of a student's welfare and still be positive with discipline. For some students school is the significant place where they feel safer, more secure and have some caring, stable adults around them.

6   Behaviour can be the *result of BDS* caused by tiredness, friendship hassles, hunger, sickness, loss and so on. Thoughtful teachers will recognise those situations and allow for them, 'Lisa, you're not normally like this—what's the problem?' They will allow cool-off time, and a chance to explain as the case may be. At the very least they will acknowledge how the student might be feeling and offer support.

7   Behaviour can be *changed*. Behaviour is not totally static and fixed. Students can learn new and different ways of relating, responding and coping in social settings, with their formal schooling and with situations of conflict. They can also learn from the kind of discipline we exercise and the modelling we offer as teachers.

8 Behaviour is *taught*. In the myriad of interactions engaged in each day at school both students and teachers are learning about behaviour. At times we will be seeking to directly influence and teach students by and through our behaviour, such as how we line them up in the corridor (in fact we can't line them up, they line up—or not as the case may be—in response to our behaviour as they perceive it). At other times we will be seeking to influence their behaviour indirectly through the teacher-student relationship. We cannot simply, easily or quickly *control* others. The art and skill of behaviour management is to lead and guide others, so that it feels to the managed that they are making the behavioural choices. Our aim is that this guiding process will lead to self-reflective and self-directed behaviour that is considerate of others.

Case study

It was a science lesson in Year 7 (copper sulphate crystals). I was team teaching several times throughout the introductory phase of the lesson. Alex called out and made silly remarks (for example, 'What are we doing this for anyway? This is dumb! We did it in Year 5'). I *tactically* ignored most of his foray into 'notice-me' behaviours. It wasn't easy as I had to keep the rest of the class on track as well. He tapped with his pencil a few times. I motioned with my hand downwards, hardly looking at him. He'd slow down for a while and repeat it. Some of his audience giggled, watching me as well as watching him. When he blatantly turned and started a private conversation while I was talking to the group, I paused and directed him to face the front and listen. He replied with a laconic sarcasm, 'Yeah, well, I was listening, wasn't I?'

Later in the on-task phase of the lesson he wandered aimlessly around the room and a couple of times into the laboratory presentation room. My colleague was getting frustrated—as was I. Thankfully almost all of the students were on-task and needed only encouragement with some refocusing; they were used to him. We had the class working in groups of three. Had it not been for that fact, I would have used time-out earlier in the lesson. But at least I knew what Alex was doing in terms of his behavioural goal: 'Notice ME!' (seeking constant attention). I suspected, too, that it was borderline power seeking: 'You can't make me settle down and work.' Apparently he was used to doing this in science. This was the first time I'd taken this Year 7 group.

I decided to direct him out of the room for some brief time-out. I suspected, though, he wouldn't go. I thought that he would set up a power struggle (a win–lose context) or he'd start a wasted-energy argument, typical of power-seeking students, for example 'Why do I have to go? I wasn't the only one! You're picking on me!'

I went outside the room for a few seconds (where the students bags were placed against the corridor wall) and said in a loud voice, 'I wonder if Alex has any writing paper in his bag.' I had said this because Alex said he couldn't do the work because he didn't have any paper. It was a ruse to get him out of the room for a few minutes. He came out like a shot and said, 'You're touching my bag!'

Away from his immediate audience, he was more settled now. I briefly described his behaviour and gave the immediate choice: work quietly until recess or leave for 'time-out'. He grumbled, I refocused and we went in. He sat and sulked and did virtually nothing. At recess I directed him to stay back along with another student. He yelled at me and kicked the wall, but he stayed back. I explained what had happened. I then directed both students to complete the set written work. Alex finished the diagram (roughly written) and then said, 'Can I go now?' I said, 'I'd like to check the work first, Alex.' (It's not easy staying calm when students are displaying hostile body language and tone.)

He ripped up the work in front of me, threw it up in the air and walked off—swearing under his breath. I knew now it was power, not just attention. I didn't chase him (that's a waste of time but I did follow up later in another colleague's class—p 96).

Eventually we set up a year-level plan for Alex. It took time and school-wide planning. Alex was one of half a dozen behaviourally disordered students for whom no *school-wide* plan had been made. Teachers were basically left to do their own thing—some were more successful than others. The problem was that Alex was clearly a catalyst for a number of other students. The plan included:
- working with Alex one to one, especially looking at reasons for his behaviour regarding attention and power seeking (p 115)
- improving follow-up and follow-through procedures (p 84)
- having a clear consequential chain (p 91)
- following a well-organised tracking procedure across classes
- developing a school-wide time-out plan (p 90)—this was crucial in the early stages of the plan
- working one to one with Alex over several weeks (and a number of sessions) to help him come to terms with his behaviour, its effect on others and the effect on his mother at home.

The elements of this individual behaviour management plan were set up by a contract supervisor who acted on behalf of all the subject teachers by:
- developing the plan with the student
- teaching the skills within the plan
- communicating with support personnel and administration
- giving the student ongoing feedback and evaluating the plan.

Alex was withdrawn from a couple of subject areas for a few weeks (initially for safety), but in time he settled back into a reasonable school existence. He is still at school. The relative success of this approach was due to the fact that it was *whole-school* in its implementation. Like all such programs it was labour-intensive but we actually spent less time overall than the approaches we had been using (initially) teacher by teacher.

Developing an individual behaviour management plan with behaviourally disordered students

There is a small percentage of students in most school populations whose behaviour severely affects the rights of teacher(s) and students. In some schools this may be up to 5% (see Wragg 1989; Rogers 1994). These students are often resistant, or show no significant response, to the teacher's classroom establishment of rights, responsibilities and rules. After-class chats, use of consequences, detention and so on may see little or no changes in the *pattern* of their disruptive behaviour.

These students are often referred to as behaviourally disordered (BD), that is, their behaviour is disordered to an inappropriate degree relative to student behaviour in the 'normal range'. Often it is necessary to develop an individual behaviour management plan (IBMP) for these students.

One of the first steps in setting up any program or plan for BD students is to have a school-wide assessment of the student's behavioural profile.

Behaviour profile

Some students may have a clinical label to their behaviour, for example, ADHD (p 118). The real issue for teachers on a day-by-day management basis, however, is to assess the student's behaviour in terms of the following:

- *Frequency:* How frequently does the student call out, seat wander, push in line, butt in, avoid a task, refuse a task and so on?
- *Intensity:* Calling out, rolling on the mat, seat leaning and so on are all annoying when they are frequent; when they are intense in their expression they are significantly more stressful for the teacher.
- *Generality:* Teachers will need to assess if a student's disruptive behaviour pattern is situation specific (associated with one teacher or subject area) or generally disruptive with all the teachers who work with that student.
- *Duration:* Is the behaviour consistently disruptive Monday to Friday, or is the behaviour worse on particular days (for example, on Mondays)? Has the student's behaviour improved with the onset of the teacher's establishment process?

It can help if teachers keep note of frequency of behaviours in their classes to give feedback to the team meeting. It is important to keep ongoing records for case conferences, departmental meetings, suspension and inquiry procedures.

If it is only one subject teacher who finds a BD student a problem, senior staff would normally work with that particular teacher and student. Is it a personality issue? Is there a need to do some conflict resolution? Is it the subject area? Does the behaviour issue with this teacher demonstrate a need for some kind of individual education plan or at least some catering for the student's differential ability?

Early intervention is essential where an unsatisfactory behaviour profile is noted across subject areas. It is important that staff work together on an IBMP. The emphasis with all behaviour planning for BD students is to approach the issue with *colleague support*, even if just one or two teachers are struggling with a student's behaviour. This involves the following:

- No blame is attached to particular teachers. The team takes a problem-solving approach.
- Where the BD student's behaviour affects several teachers across the year level, it is important to have a *year-level plan* rather than an English teacher's plan or maths teacher's plan. This plan is more than a behaviour monitoring card which, of course, has its place with some students. An IBMP aims to both *track* and *teach* a BD student across subject areas. Sometimes the student's behaviour significantly affects all teachers across a year level.
- Make sure there is a year-level, faculty-supported (even school-wide), time-out plan (p 90). This plan needs a crisis-management option for situations where the BD student is effectively holding a class to (psychological) ransom. This back-up plan needs to be simple, workable and tied in with positive follow-up by any teacher who initiates time-out.
- Call a year-level meeting of all the teachers who teach the BD student. Although this discussion is time consuming, it is worthwhile. After a whinge from colleagues, it is important to get down to a problem-solving and action-planning approach. Discuss the student's behaviour profile. Share background information (accessible within ethical probity) that can affect an understanding of the student's behaviour. Discuss basics such as who the student sits with, whether behaviour is better or worse on particular days and in particular subject areas, and whether behaviour is worse during on-task time or instructional time. Find out if are there any approaches being used that staff have found effective. It is important to discuss discipline approaches with such students. Teachers who rely on confrontational/authoritarian approaches frequently struggle with the management of BD students.

Contract supervision and case-management

It is necessary to select a contract supervisor (CS). Consider who on staff is best suited to set up the behaviour plan on behalf of their subject colleagues. This person (often the year-level supervisor) will need to have good communication skills, experience of working with challenging students and some skill at working with students on setting goals for change and monitoring changes (in this case behaviour change). Most of all the CS will need some extra time-release to set up the behaviour plans with profiled students. See Figure 7.1.

You're not our normal teacher!

FIGURE 7.1
CASE MANAGEMENT

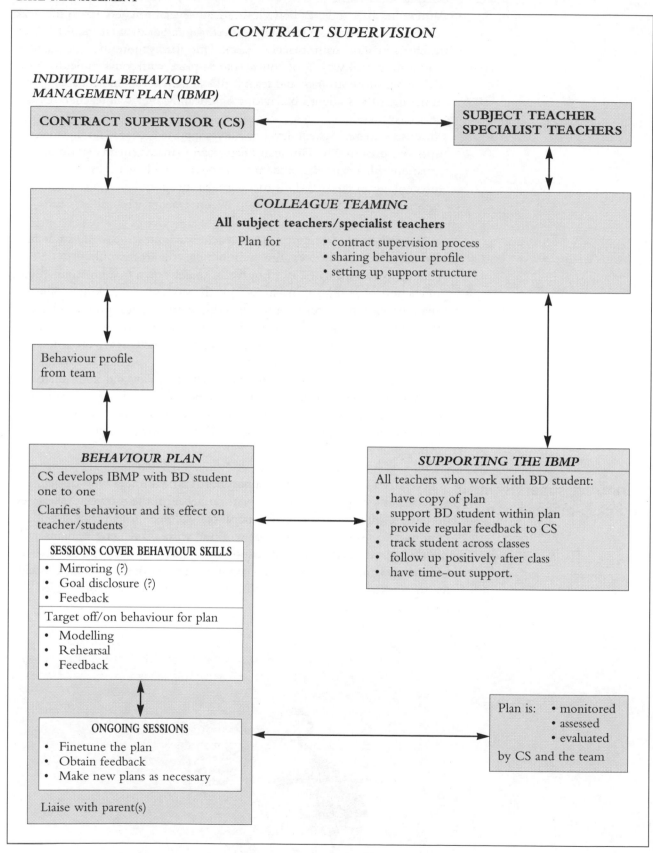

At primary level the contract supervision will normally be carried out by the Year teacher, unless that teacher is so disaffected by the child's behaviour that any one-to-one work would be counterproductive (that teacher having lost the emotional and psychological goodwill). Because the year teacher has such a significant classroom-based relationship with the student, any IBMP would need their significant input, especially in terms of linking the one-to-one sessions with encouragement back in the classroom setting.

The CS (sometimes called 'case manager') will:
• liaise with all subject teachers at the student's year level
• liaise with other personnel on staff or support staff (for example, community liaison officer or social worker as may be necessary)
• liaise with administration on a regular basis and call any subsequent meetings with parents or teachers, and attend any suspension procedures or case conferences
• set up a behaviour plan with the BD student based on discussion of the student's behaviour as it is affecting fundamental rights of teachers and students.

As with all one-to-one sessions with a student, it is important for the CS to consider the following:
• The location of the area where they will be working with the student needs careful thought. Are there teachers nearby? Is the area visible from the outside but still giving workable privacy? If there's no glass door should you leave the exit door ajar? (Yes)
• The length of each session should be considered.
• It is especially important that when a male CS works with a female student over a 20- to 30-minute session, a female colleague also be present (abstractedly in the background doing her work program or whatever). It might be more appropriate and effective for a female colleague to work with a female student as CS, especially considering the background of some of our students.

Context for behaviour planning

The *context* for all behaviour planning is the basic rights and responsibilities inherent in the school's behaviour policy. The *aim* of any behaviour plan is to increase the student's:
• *self-awareness* of their behaviour and how it is affecting their own learning
• *self-control and behaviour ownership*.
In developing a plan the student is encouraged to work on academic survival skills and social survival skills at school. Basic academic survival skills include how to get teacher attention during up-front instructional time and on-task learning time, how to initiate and sustain a learning task, how to communicate frustration about a learning issue, having basic equipment, having a work schedule and doing one's best (always give a structure for the concept of 'doing one's best'). Basic social skills include how to enter and leave a classroom without causing hassles, how to find a seat and stay in it, how to keep hands and feet to oneself, how to use basic social cues such as 'please' and 'can I borrow?', how to put things back in their place or return them to their owner, and how to move around the classroom (and when it's appropriate to move around

in given subject areas) without annoying others—this is linked to the concept of staying on task (an issue that is particularly difficult for ADHD students).

In developing an IBMP with a student, the emphasis is not on counselling but on teaching the skills of behaviour ownership at school. It is owning one's own behaviour in a way that considers *others'* rights and the specific skills necessary to that end. The focus, then, is primarily *educational*.

Of course, an effective CS develops positive relationships quickly with such students and will be party from time to time to information from school counsellors and social workers. In the one-to-one sessions, however, the CS's role is primarily to help the student with their behaviour through reskilling rather than getting locked into causative mitigation ('I can't behave well because I come from a dysfunctional home!'). CSs will emphasise that a person's difficult home background or life's circumstances *contribute* to ineffective and stressful behaviour, but they don't *cause* that behaviour.

It is important to point out to the student: 'No one *makes* you kick a chair in the classroom, call out frequently, come late to class, argue with your teachers, swear at teachers or refuse to do work you know you can actually do.' The CS can say, 'There are different things you can do when you're uptight, frustrated or even angry. I want to help you with a plan for your behaviour so you don't keep getting into hassles with your teachers and parent(s). Your behaviour is your choice. However, that doesn't mean that the choices are easy—they are often hard.'

In all conversations about behaviour the CS is supportive and gives descriptive feedback about behaviour (rather than judging the student). The emphasis is always: 'We like you but we don't like some of your behaviours because . . . [always refer to the *context*—the basic non-negotiable rights and responsibilities]. Your behaviour is sometimes unacceptable [the rights-affecting behaviour], wrong or bad, not *you*.' It is psychologically unnecessary (though tempting) to say, 'You are a bad *person*.'

The process of developing a behaviour plan is much the same whatever the age of the student:
- a one-to-one context over time
- an adult mentor with back-up mentoring, where appropriate, from the student's peer (primary-age level)
- simplicity
- focus on the student's present behaviour(s) but with a view to immediate and ongoing change
- starting with a few behaviours at a time: off-task to on-task
- using multiple entry points such as mirroring, picture cues, goal disclosure (p 115), modelling, rehearsal feedback and ongoing evaluation (Figure 7.1).

Sessions covering behaviour skills

Most students will need several sessions with their CS.

Session One will concentrate on the reasons for the student being in the position of having to be on a behaviour plan. It can help if the CS describes the behaviours specifically affecting the student's learning (and other students' rights, including the teacher's right to teach). The disclosure can be enhanced by some gentle mirroring (p 88) of the main troublesome and disturbing behaviours.

Ask supplementary questions such as:
- How often do you think you speak like that (or call out or butt in)? Refer the student to your frequency count.
- How do you think other students feel or are affected by . . . ? When students are invited to give feedback they often (not always but often) do the following:
  —Shift blame: 'Yeah, well, I'm not the only one!' or 'What about Jason and that! He calls out and stuff!'
  —Excuse their behaviour:'Yeah, well, I don't do that all the time' or 'Yeah, well I hate this subject!'
  —Globalise the issues (a form of escape): 'All the teachers here couldn't give a sh–t!' or 'I hate this school.'
  —Adopt provocative avoidance tactics: 'Yeah, well, I don't care!' or 'So?' (this is a brief, apparent couldn't-care-less approach expressed in a single word). One of my standard responses to the 'I don't care' comments is to add 'but I care, Jason—so do most teachers here'.

Refocus the student by disputing, clarifying and getting back to the issue at hand (the student's behaviour). Refer to the right or rule and the student's affecting of the fundamental safety, treatment and learning of others.

The following activities may be carried out in the sessions:
- *Use picture cues* (primary and lower secondary). My colleagues and I have found that simple drawings (cartoon style) can give another entry point into students' understanding about their behaviour (Rogers 1994). Picture cues are particularly helpful at lower secondary level or for students whose communication/dialogue skills are not as focused as those of other students. It gives the student something to look at and refer to *while* the teacher is speaking. The picture cues portray the key *off-task* (disruptive) behaviour(s), the social disapproval of student and teacher, and the on-task behaviour with corresponding social approval.

The teacher converses with the student 'through' the pictures:

Teacher: 'Who do you think this person here is?' Giving a wry smile, the teacher points to the student in the picture calling out, butting in or seat wandering.

Student: 'Is that supposed to be me?' (I've heard that response a number of times.)

Teacher: 'Best drawing I could do.'

Teacher: 'What are you doing in the picture?'

The teacher can now refer to both off-task and on-task pictures to gain an understanding of where the student is now and where the student needs to be if they want to change their behaviour.

- *Target a few key behaviours*. The teacher discusses with the student behaviours they will need to stop (and why) and behaviours they will need to start (and why). This can be done through picture cues or writing it down. Preferably target just two or three behaviours, and keep the language specific, simple and behaviourally focused. For example, 'If you need teacher help in work time, put up your hand and wait, but remember to check the work carefully first or quietly check with a class mentor.' It can be helpful for more restless students if they have an ancillary work task(s) to go on with while they wait for their teacher to give personal assistance. It can also help to ask the BD student if there is a student in their class(es) whom they would be comfortable to accept support from with the plan (primary level). Offer one or two names of students who would be willing to act as peer mentors (Rogers 1994). The teacher would need to have checked beforehand with the persons whose names are offered. It would be important to discuss with nominated mentors what their role would be, especially how to remind and to encourage (not to force). It is helpful if the mentor sits with (or on the same table as) the BD student. Change the mentor role if the mentor gets fed up or too hassled.

- *Model the target behaviours*. For example, the teacher models how loud is a quiet-working voice or partner voice. The teacher also models how to line up without pushing or shoving, enter the room and get teacher attention appropriately. Whether the student should have a 'set seat' in some subject areas should have already been discussed with other staff members. The student should be told to sit away from students who will hassle or get the student into trouble. This will need to be planned with each teacher as necessary. The significance of modelling should not be underestimated. Some students, especially at primary age level, may not have been *specifically* taught time-on-task behaviour, or how (and why) to get teacher attention appropriately. See Figure 7.2.

FIGURE 7.2

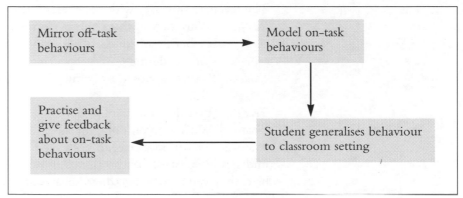

- *Rehearse the behaviour plan.* The CS invites the student to do a dummy run: 'OK, your turn now, Ahmed. Give me a demo of how you're going to enter the room' (or ask a question, speak quietly during work time, stay on-task and so on). If the student feels too much of a 'dag' or just refuses (it happens sometimes), remodel the behaviour and invite the student verbally to go over the plan with you. Most students will have a go at practising.
- *Discuss the bad-day syndrome* (BDS). Ask the student: 'What will you do if you are having a really bad day and are feeling like . . . ?' With the student make up a frustration–tolerance plan: count backwards from *10*, breathe in and out slowly five times, ask to go out for a drink, or write down 'what's hassling me' to show it to their CS later. If it's a particular teacher that the student perceives is bugging them, discuss how the student can approach the teacher later, after class, to make their feelings clear. Rehearse some of the things they could say—these could be written down on the back of the behaviour contract plan. Some students will be helped by having a specific session or two on anger management (Rogers 1994). Point out the difference between a BDS (we all have these, especially mums, dads and teachers) and *characteristic* behaviours such as bad temper, tantrums and 'spitting the dummy'. Say, 'On bad days let the teacher know, quietly, that you're having a bad day and use your personal *plan*. Tell yourself, "I'm getting really annoyed" and then remember your plan: "I can calm myself by . . ." Now, let's go over it again. I'll show you how and then we'll write it down.' Point out that, as with any new skill (or new/different way of doing things), we have slip-ups or bad days, and that the students need to recognise that and learn from it, but stick with the plan. I find it helpful to talk about something the student is proficient at (say in sport or hobbies) and ask how they got better at it. The student generally replies, 'By practice, effort, going back over it, and doing it until it becomes sort of second nature.'

'Publish' the plan in a user-friendly form. This can be through simple descriptions of behaviours (as goals) or off-task and on-task behaviours (Appendix 3). List any idiosyncratic caveats such as: 'On my bad days I'll let my teacher know by having a quiet word on the way into class.'

Make sure each subject teacher or specialist gets a copy of the plan (exactly as given to the student) so that the subject teacher can refer to the plan with the student for both support and discipline. It is important that all subject teachers are supportive of the student's plan. I've seen really good efforts by a student damaged by a few teachers who won't make the effort to be supportive by being positive with the student and quietly referring to the plan when disciplining the student who is off-task (and off-plan). For example, 'David, what's your plan for . . . ?', or 'What should you be doing according to your plan?'.

It is important to stress to subject teachers that the student in question is not getting special privileges by being on an individual behaviour plan. Rather, the student is being given individual *support* (in much the same way as a student with any special needs has a plan, for example an individual education plan).

BD students are subject to the same discipline (and consequences) that any student has to face when overly disruptive. What is hoped is that all teachers will support the school-wide emphasis on:

- positive correction
- supportive follow-up and follow-through
- related consequences
- encouragement.

The consistent support of subject teachers is essential to the success of any IBMP.

If the student refuses any one-to-one assistance from a CS, it is pointless pushing the concept of an IBMP. Even if it is written up the student won't 'own' it, and ownership is an important part of the program.

The CS can point out that, if the student continues to behave in the ways noted (revisit, *specifically*, the disruptive behaviours at issue), there is a chain of consequences the school will have to use. Point out: 'This is not because we dislike you but because we can't allow you to continually call out (wander, push in and so on)'. You can add, 'However, my door is always open to work on a plan to help you with your behaviour.' If the student responds with another, 'I don't give a . . . !', calmly point out, 'But I do and so do your parent(s).' (At least you hope they do.)

By outlining the consequences (continued time-out, possible suspension, continued parent contact and so on), the CS is putting the responsibility back where it belongs—on the student—but always with the genuine caveat that support, long-term support, is available for behaviour change. It is also important for the students to get the message that their behaviour is their choice. The CS's job is, in part, to support the student with the skills to make better behavioural choices.

Evaluating the program— a case study

Some students respond quickly to the concept of a personal behaviour plan. Chris, an ADHD child in Year 3, was constantly rolling on the mat and making silly noises during mat time. He also found it difficult to stay in his seat during on-task learning time.

In the first session the grade teacher (CS) used picture cues (p 109) and some gentle mirroring (p 88) to clarify his current, typical behaviour. She asked Chris how many times he thought he called out and rolled around, and she referred to the mirroring she had just done ('just like that') and the picture. The student was pretty close to the mark when he said, 'About 10 times?', to which the teacher replied, 'Actually 15, Chris.'

The CS didn't waste any time with exploring why he rolled on the mat and called out. She invited Chris to work on a plan to help him sit on the mat (like the others) and put up his hand without calling out. She explained why these behaviours were important and referred to the effect of his (present) behaviour on other children. Using the picture (below) of the student engaging in off-task behaviour, she referred to the sad faces of the children near him.

Chris responded by saying they were sad because he was 'not listening to the teacher' and 'moving around too much'. The CS then showed Chris a second picture with him on-task (sitting on the mat with his hand up) with corresponding social approval in the faces on his peers. One of the benefits of the plan is that it can increase social/peer approval. This is especially important with ADHD children who are often alienated from positive peer approval, though of course they may often receive inappropriate and negative peer attention. The concept of social approval can be discussed with children of any age in terms of the fundamental rights of everyone being enhanced when the student behaves consistently with their plan.

After modelling the new behaviour (twice), the CS invited Chris to practise the plan (twice). She gave him feedback and encouragement. She also gave him a small copy of the 'plan' they had been using in the session (reduced from A4). She asked him where he'd like to keep his copy. He replied, 'In my work tray.' Younger students often keep their copy on their class table (it is their choice). Over the first few days Chris increased his on-task behaviours (sitting on the mat without rolling around or calling out, and putting up his hand without calling out when he wanted to ask a question or make a comment). The approximations of his behaviour to what he had practised in the one-to-one sessions were noted as a tick in the boxes at the bottom of his *reminder plan*. When he left the mat to work at his table the CS quickly called him back and asked him to get his 'plan'. She encouraged him by saying (with a smile), 'You remembered your plan. Let's put a tick on your plan and on my copy too.'

In subsequent sessions the CS worked on a plan to help Chris stay on task at his seat, including work-task cards for key learning times (p 120). She also worked on a simple plan to help with his loudness of voice in class and tied in this individual plan with the whole-class noise monitoring plan (p 70). The CS made sure all the specialist teachers, teacher aides and the administration had a copy of the plan and a note on how she was using the plan in class.

What teachers need to recognise is that it takes most students some time to develop new patterns of behaviour and the attitude changes that go with the process of behaviour change. It is also important to see that success is *realistically* measured in a reduction in frequency and intensity of disruptive behaviour and an increase in generality of on-task behaviour over time.

Teachers should be considerate of the efforts students make with their plan and treat bad days as bad days. They should not discount progress with the plan because the student has a 'bad' or 'off day'. On those days the normal (and fair) process of discipline needs to be exercised. If teachers want perfection they are wanting what is unrealistic—even some of the 'good' students are disruptive from time to time.

Subsequent sessions

In all subsequent sessions the contract supervisor and the student should do the following:
- Discuss how the plan is going in respective classes (what is working well and why, and areas where the plan needs to be finetuned or modified).
- Refine or add elements to the plan or make new plans as necessary.
- Go over old and new skills, especially those challenging the student's beliefs: 'It's too hard!', 'It's not worth it!' or 'What does it matter anyway?'.
- Discuss teacher feedback to/from various classes. The student may need help dealing with what they perceive to be unfair or unsupportive teachers. It may be necessary to develop some skills of how to speak to a teacher after class and the sorts of things that could be said when wanting to make a complaint or share a concern.
- The CS may well have to revisit old behaviour through mirroring (p 88) and goal disclosure (p 115) as well as set up more practice sessions.

It is important to give feedback to the parent/s (caregiver) about how the program is going. Most parents are very supportive—some are only too glad the school is 'doing something' (because they may feel powerless, or feel that nothing they do matters).

A home–school diary or a special letter to outline the positive outcomes their child is making can elicit the secondary encouragement that the home environment can provide. It is probably better to make sure that any negative feedback is given in person at a school meeting so that the principal (and CS) can give such feedback in context to minimise it being misconstrued.

I have had case conferences with parents regarding their BD offspring where the following comments were made:
- 'He was all right at the last fifteen schools!'
- 'Just do what I do—give him a good smack! Never did me any harm!'
- 'You're just picking on my son!'

Giving feedback to authoritarian/hostile/suspicious or jaded parents is not easy. Keeping them focused on the child's present behaviour and taking a *supportive* approach that allows for corrective consequential discipline is the purpose of a parent–teacher meeting. The meeting is not an opportunity to blame the parents (tempting as that may be on some occasions). We emphasise what we've found helpful and why, and what the school is doing with respect to behaviour and why. Then we invite parental support.

Goal disclosure

Goal disclosure (Dreikurs et al 1982) is a technique designed to help students better understand their disruptive behaviour. According to Rudolf Dreikurs, behaviour is *purposeful and goal-directed*. These behaviour 'goals' enable students to feel that they 'belong' to the social group. When students are disruptive they may well be pursuing goals within the social context. When a boy repeatedly calls out instead of putting up his hand, his need for attention is met—this is his *goal* ('I belong when my teacher and/or the class is frequently noticing and attending to me'). In the student's private logic, he perceives that this is how to get attention. This does not mean the student is fully aware of what is happening (especially with infant-aged children), but, if a teacher or parent constantly reinforces inappropriate attention seeking, the association still confirms (in the child's perception) that this is how the need for attention (belonging) is met.

Goal-directed behaviours

Dreikurs has identified several goal-directed behaviours adopted by students in order to belong to the social group:

*   *Attention* seeking may take the form of constant clowning, and silly and nuisance behaviours. Teachers may overservice, over-remind or coax some students, but at the same time become irritated and frustrated, and resent the amount of time taken up by these students.
*   *Power* seeking may take the form of stubborn, often argumentative, challenging behaviour and disobedience. Teachers may feel threatened and angry at the pressure this puts on their leadership (and status position).
*   *Revenge* seeking may take the form of destructive behaviour and often involves accusing or blaming others of unfairness. Teachers may feel hurt and may even want to hurt back.
*   Feelings of *inadequacy* may take the form of students giving up easily and not participating. Teachers will often feel discouraged in their difficulty in reaching the student.

These reactions by some teachers are natural and not easy to retrain. In the short term it may be helpful to think about how some behaviours can be tactically ignored, how some behaviours can be redefined (for example, power struggles), how best to avoid overservicing their attention or power seeking or overly cajoling students, and how to use humour (not sarcasm) to defuse tension and turn situations around. Avoid punitive and reactive styles of behaviour management (p 15/16).

Disclosing the goal

Disclosing the 'goal' can be done in the following way:

*   In a one-to-one session with the student, the teacher needs to pursue several questions with the student to raise awareness of the student's *purposeful*, but mistaken, goals.
*   Plan, *ahead of time*, the key questions and likely reactions from the student.
*   Set the tone to be supportive and invitational. It is essential that the whole goal-disclosure process not be seen by the student as another detention or punishment session. It is, effectively, part of the total

repairing and rebuilding process.
- It can help to use picture cues or some gentle mirroring (p 88) to set the scene (Rogers 1994).
- Goal disclosure needs to consider a child's age and understanding.

Key questions

The key questions are designed to focus on what the child is trying to achieve through their behaviour. Dreikurs makes the point that these questions need to be phrased as considered 'guesses'. At no point do we say: 'I know why you do . . . ' Say instead: 'Do you know why . . . ?' The purpose of the 'why' question is to prepare for the subsequent questions.

Dreikurs suggests the following procedure: Present the student with their 'goal' in the form of a question such as 'Could it be that . . .?' The teacher then follows with the references to the specific goal: 'Could it be that when you call out many times in class you want the class (and me) to notice you a lot?' The phrase 'Could it be' is not an accusation; it is only a guess that may be correct or incorrect. If it is incorrect, we should 'guess' again (Dreikurs et al 1982, p 30).

The following questions have been adapted from Dreikurs et al (1982, pp 29–32):

1 *Attention:* 'Could it be that . . .
   - you want to keep me busy with you and your requests?
   - you want me to notice you more? Help you more?
   - you want the rest of the class to notice you?/laugh at you when . . . ?
   - you want to keep the group/class busy with you?
   - you want to be special to the group?'
2 *Power:* 'Could it be that . . .
   - you want to show me that you can do what you want and that we can't stop you?
   - you want to do what you want to do *when* you want to do it—and that no one can (really) stop you?
   - you want to be the boss—you want to be in charge—the one "calling the shots"?'
   Remember, the tone is questioning and 'guessing', not judgmental or pejorative.
3 *Revenge:* 'Could it be that . . .
   - you want to get back at . . . , pay back. . . , get even for . . . ?
   - you want to hurt me, get even with me for . . .? [or] You want to hurt him (name . . .) or her (name . . .)?
   - you want to show me that I cannot get away with . . . ? [for example punishing, contacting parents, notifying the principal . . .]
   - you want to make me (or the class or . . .) feel bad or feel hurt?'
4 *Display of inadequacy:* 'Could it be that . . .
   - you want to be left alone because you can't do anything? You're afraid to fail?
   - you can't be on top, the winner, first?
   - you want me to stop asking you questions or trying to make you work?

- you feel you don't know the answers in class and you don't want the other students to know?
- you feel insignificant [explain] unless you can always succeed . . . be the best in whatever you do . . . or always get it right?
- you feel you must never make mistakes (in your work, in sport, in school)?'

In pursuing the questions it is important to pace the process and go through the sequence beginning with attention onwards. If the teacher suspects borderline power, say, rather than attention, it is worth pursuing the disclosure on power. These questions form the framework for how the teacher could approach the issue of disclosures. Dreikurs gives a range in his book. For example, take passive power (what some teachers regard as dumb insolence): 'Could it be that you are not talking in order to frustrate me (and others) and make me feel helpless and defeated?' or 'Could it be that you are willing to do anything in order to feel a big shot?'

Completing the goal disclosure

In responding to the disclosure, the younger student may involuntarily agree with the teacher. Most students will demonstrate some acknowledgment such as a smile, embarrassed laughter or pulling a face. Dreikurs calls this the 'recognition reflex'. Older students will also give away some non-verbal agreement or recognition even if they say 'no'—their mouths twitch, their seating posture shows discomfort or they look away and up.

The questioning process is designed to enable insight and recognition for the student. After the response I find it helpful with older children to partially agree with the student's private logic and goal. If you are dealing with power seeking, you can say: 'Well, I can't really *stop* you being boss . . . or *make* you do the work . . . or *make* you like me or any of your teachers. I need your help and co-operation to change things.'

We need to frame our language and approach relative to the age of the student. I would encourage the use of picture cues, mirroring and modelling as educational entry points into the student's understanding, especially at primary level. It is important to also point out that their behaviour is not accidental—it is learned and they can relearn with our help.

We make an offer to the student to work on a plan with the teacher as a way of helping the student to do better at school in terms of their academic work and behaviour (also such a plan can help to keep the student out of trouble).

Some very helpful programs for older students who are behaviourally disordered have been developed by Wragg (1989). These programs and plans, he points out, need to have a voluntary commitment by the student in order to be effective. This is important with adolescents simply because without voluntary co-operation and effort by the student, the plan will not work anyway. Some students will tacitly agree to work on a program to stay out of trouble but attitudinally refuse to go in for the long haul.

Wragg's program (1989) also offers a range of approaches designed to skill the student in talking sense to himself/herself (Rogers 1994 for a program for primary-aged students). It is important when developing behaviour plans to consider the issue of self-talk (self-guiding speech), how it affects behaviour and how teachers can teach students to challenge and 'dispute' erroneous demanding and globalised thinking. ('*All* teachers are idiots', 'I *hate* school', '*No one* here cares', '. . . *can't* change things'.) Reframing is a skill students need to learn as part of human development programs generally.

If the student is repeatedly unwilling to make a plan (p 112), point out the ongoing consequences, and the effect on school work and on home life. Of course, *some* students may be acting up at school in order to get the attention of their parents or even to 'get back' at their parents (Glasser 1991). Goal disclosure can be helpful here as a way of exposing this issue, coming to terms with it and offering appropriate support (Dreikurs et al 1982).

Behaviours associated with attention deficit disorder

Teachers at every level of education are now familiar with the 'disorder of the decade'—attention deficit disorder—ADD (or ADHD where the hyperactive factor is dominant). Countless popular articles have been written about children with ADD. I have spoken with some teachers who have labelled typical physical restlessness and lack of concentration as ADD behaviour, even when the student has never been diagnosed with the disorder. It is very important that a student be correctly diagnosed before being labelled as ADD. That diagnosis is best carried out by a clinical psychologist or a paediatrician working with the school and parent(s). I've heard a teacher comment: 'Half my class is ADD! And some of the male teachers are too!'

The typical symptoms of ADD and ADHD are quoted as:
- Inattention, overactivity, physical restlessness, instability, impulsiveness and social clumsiness may be signs of ADD (and delayed social development may be a sign of ADD).
- ADD-diagnosed children often find it difficult to concentrate or focus on learning tasks and are very easily distracted.
- A lack of task focus in ADD children is exacerbated by the fact they often appear as disorganised, and are inattentive and impulsive (at times recklessly impulsive).
- ADD-diagnosed children consequently often have low self-esteem because they may well be shunned by their immediate class peers who get fed up with their behaviour in class (or in the playground). As *Time* magazine notes: 'They are the kids no one wants at a birthday party' (*Time*, 5 September 1994).

If you have a child/adolescent diagnosed with ADD in your classes (and odds on you will), they may be on medication, normally Ritalin or dexamphetamine (Dexetrine). Many ADD children are helped by medication (but not all). Medication assists the condition (in terms of focus, concentration and slowing down physical restlessness). Some parents and doctors swear by these medications and many teachers will testify the difference it makes in some (diagnosed) ADD children's behaviour (see especially Serfontein 1990; Green & Chee 1995). What medication cannot do, however, is teach children what to do with any new-found behavioural focus; they will still need a behaviour plan.

A behaviour plan—an individual behaviour plan—can teach the student the academic and social skills needed to cope and achieve at school. While the taking and supporting of medication maybe an important part of ADD management, the student will also need to learn the essential basic self-coping skills.

As part of any recovery plan (Rogers 1994), teachers will need to consider the following aspects of the classroom environment:
- Be careful to organise seating where ADD students can see the chalkboard, they are near the teacher and they are with a classmate (or classmates) who is a positive and helpful role model. Some students will benefit from having a target student as a 'plan helper'. This is a student

who is nominated and is willing to support the BD child with their behaviour plan and on-task learning.

- Be aware that ADD students are visual learners. Write on the chalkboard or give written instructions rather than just relying on auditory learning. This is why picture cueing can be effective in developing specific behaviour plans (Rogers 1994). Because of short-term memory problems, even visual cues for rules and routines can help.

- Assist the student with time-management tasks. Teach clock-related time-on-task to enable the student to get a sense of how long the diary writing and so on would *normally* take. Time-task cards can also be beneficial where the child has daily task cards that outline the specific learning task and also give a time breakdown of the task. This helps to make a longer task seem more achievable.

- Many ADD students do not write quickly or correctly. It can help to have written notes or allow the ADD student to copy from another student. The student ticks off the time allocation relative to the task.

- It can help to make sure the ADD student's desk is uncluttered and kept clear of distracters. It will help the student to have a well-organised routine and structure to their day (even written up with simple cartoons at lower-middle primary). In Special Schools, photos and time allocations provide visual checks and benchmarks for a student's daily routine. For homework tasks, use a homework book so the student can paste in their worksheets.

- Have a personal checklist and train the ADD student to check through the list before going home.

- Because of the ADD student's natural physical restlessness it can be helpful to build the option of movement into the plan. For example, after 10 minutes on their work plan the student takes it over to the teacher to have a look (this quiet movement gives a brief, purposeful release from sitting). Wherever possible give some movement/monitor role to the ADD student. Avoid overuse of recess times as a consequence for ADD students—they need the physical exercise/release that playtimes bring.

- Keep encouraging the student with descriptive feedback (p 78). Where possible give such feedback close to the effort(s).
- Use positive discipline practices.

The most important point about working with diagnosed ADD students is that we have a whole-school approach. If necessary there will need to be a common school-wide individual behaviour plan. Even if a student is not diagnosed as ADD, the practices noted here are relevant for children with symptomatic ADD behaviour—these children too will benefit from individual plans.

At primary level it would be worth putting even several students on an individual behaviour/learning plan if the frequency and intensity of their behaviour is well outside the normal range (Rogers 1994). While it may seem like a lot of work at the outset it is worth it over the long term.

Staff will need to be reminded that a special plan with such children is not excusing their behaviour—it is supporting behaviour. These students do have special needs that schools have to cater for. This does not mean they are excused normative discipline, but it does mean that any discipline is exercised within a *known plan*, making disruptive and off-task behaviour easier to manage.

Chapter 8

RELIEF TEACHERS AND THE HARD CLASS

A winner
Seeks for the goodness in a bad man
and works with that part of him.

A loser
Looks only for the badness in a good
man, and therefore finds it hard to
work with anyone.

Sydney Harris, Winner and
Losers, *1973*

'Who are you? You're not our normal teacher.' I've had that said to me many, many times when I've taken demonstration classes (classes where the regular teacher(s) sits in while I do my best to take 4E or 10L). You can always answer, 'There are no normal teachers, mate.'

Challenges facing relief teachers

It is very common for relief teachers to be challenged by students about issues of routine, work requirements and management generally. The most common statement I hear when I'm taking a class (as a demonstration teacher) is, 'Ms F lets us do "x", "y" and "z".' My standard reply is 'Maybe she does (a bit of partial agreement), but the school rule for chewing gum or hats, or . . . is . . . ' It's a waste of time arguing with the student about the veracity of what their regular teacher does or doesn't do. That is why it is helpful for relief teachers to bring a set of key rule reminders into the class with them. These rule reminders can cover areas such as:
- the fair learning rule
- the fair communication rule
  - movement around the room
  - respect in our classroom.

Relief or supply teaching has its own unique challenges where students test out, waste time and have fun with this new teacher. As one child said, 'Children who muck up for the relief teachers usually muck up for our own teacher but not as bad' (Wood & Knight 1994).

You're not our normal teacher!

A relief teacher has to go through what all teachers go through in their first encounters with a new group—the establishment phase. This is the testing out of boundaries, relationships, responses, comparisons with other teachers and so on.

It is important that relief teachers define the teaching situation for themselves and not just assume they walk into a set pattern; the pattern changes because they are there. They are new and significant players in the group dynamics; they don't merely stand in for the regular teacher. In their study on relief teachers and their initial encounters with a class, Wood and Knight (1994, 390) note that students were able to find out (through having 'fun' and 'fooling around' or 'loud mouthing') 'how much noise or lack of manners (for example, calling out) individual supply/relief teachers would tolerate and how much or how little work they would have to do'.

The most common observation (cum complaint) of relief teachers is that they believe other staff do not take them seriously, and that they are not always treated as 'real teachers'. We feel that we're 'sort of baby-sitters', 'second-class citizens' and 'not a colleague'. Students, too, may see the relief teacher merely as a supervising adult, who is there for controlling classes or revising work—not really there to teach. 'Unless the supply/relief teacher has his or her job viewed by pupils, their parents and teachers as a valuable part of teaching, not just for baby-sitting (control) purposes, then pupil expectations will remain low, as status of teachers is communicated to pupils by others.' (Wood & Knight 1994, p 392). Of course, this occurs, but it is a cause of concern that it occurs at all.

The relief teacher walks into a staffroom full of strangers—yet these people are his 'colleagues'. He reaches for a cup (he's been looking forward to a cuppa). He'll take it out with him on playground duty. (Relief teachers *always* get playground duty!) Someone says, 'That's my cup!' I've even seen teachers challenge visitors about the rights to particular chairs or seating places. I have observed countless staffrooms over the years and have seen a stranger walk in (loaded with the bits and pieces common to relief teaching) and no one has moved across to their colleague to even say 'Hi'. In some cases the body language of the regular staff indicates they don't even acknowledge the existence of their visiting colleague. When you've just had a hard class the last thing you need is this kind of petty nonsense.

What a difference it would make if the visiting teacher were to be:
• introduced by a senior colleague (briefly) to the staff
• given a cup (some relief teachers take their own just in case)
• personally introduced to a few teachers (some people are not self-starters).
If there is a teaching buddy for the day this teacher will often do these things on behalf of a senior colleague. I'm not talking about shepherding relief teachers all day—just a little bit of understanding by colleagues of how they might be feeling as newcomers.

Supporting relief teachers

Imagine the relief teacher covering 8D for several days or a relief teacher coming in to cover the challenging Year 2. They may not know anyone at the school and may have got this job via a phone call. They get to the school early (most do) and go to the office to find out exactly what's on. Sometimes the office doesn't know what class(es) this person will be taking. The time is ticking away and the relief teacher is thinking, 'I need the photocopier. I don't know my way around the school. What year (or class) have I got? Can I get there early enough to set up . . . ?' They may well be at school to cover that hard class (the possible reason for the regular teacher taking a few days off). This preys a little on the mind of relief teachers!

It is important that the office staff demonstrate basic professional courtesy to the relief teacher, not some dismissive: 'Oh, go down to so and so—he'll know where you are today.' Basic as it sounds, a 'relief teacher guide to our school' would be a helpful start. It needs to be a simple, user-friendly document (one or two pages) outlining the following information:

- Bell (recess) times should be given. This may sound basic, but times vary.
- Essential rules for that class or group being taken by the relief teacher should be supplied. Children do tend to test out any new teacher, especially a relief teacher who is *only* there for a day or two. It can help enormously at primary age level if the relief teacher is made aware of any special routines for lining up, sitting on the mat, quiet reading, lunch monitors (published by the grade teacher) and so on. It can also help at secondary level to know how the 'home' tutor group session is normally conducted.
- Have listed the key people within the team so the relief colleague can refer to it. It can help, for example, to use their regular teacher's name when referring to class rules—it makes it sound as though the relief teacher knows what is going on. The list will also include support teachers and, of course, the teaching buddy for the day. Having a teacher buddy (a colleague, in the team, teaching nearby) gives both structural security and some emotional security.
- Notification should be provided of any students on special behaviour contracts or 'daily report cards'. Note down the normal routine for checking such contracts with the student. This would normally be done privately, one to one, not saying out loud, 'I know that three students in this room are on daily report cards.'
- Notification should also be provided of any students who are on special medication or first-aid regimes plus the name of the referral person. Basic, I know, but easy to overlook.
- The exit/time-out plan should be outlined, with special reference to any particular students. (It can even help to know, in advance, some key phrases used by the regular teacher, for example: 'I normally direct Jason to time-out in this way . . .') I've seen this preventative caveat used successfully in many schools. It provides another link between the regular teacher and the new teacher. Managing a crisis situation is probably the most important structural and emotional assurance we can provide for a relief teacher—the assurance that with a hard class, back-up can and will be provided. Relief teachers will need to know how to exercise the time-out plan (p 90), who the reference colleague is and what written

reporting is necessary. Let the teacher know that the exit/time-out card (p 92) can be used as a safety-valve measure to notify a senior colleague if the class is off-the-wall, or as an exit for an individual student who it is suspected will refuse to leave the class upon the teacher's directions. Many teachers (at primary) have a file box with these essentials written out for use by relief teachers. The supervising teacher can then refer the relief teacher to this as soon as practicable that day.

- It can help (especially at primary level) to have a 4W Form available for use as the preferred option as a consequence. The 4W Form can be a link between the regular and the new teacher (p 89).
- If the school has a particular discipline plan, common to all teachers, then the relief teacher will need a user-friendly summary of it.

It can help if the supervising colleague is welcoming towards the support teacher and:
- invites the relief teacher to have a cup of tea/coffee
- shows the teacher the photocopier (gives the teacher a number)
- introduces the teaching buddy for the day
- gives the teacher a user-friendly (clear) map of the school and shades in the classroom(s) where the teacher will be that day (remember how confusing the geographical layout of your school was the first week?)
- provides a timetable (especially important if the students have a specialist teacher that day) and a playground-duty roster.

It can also be helpful if the supervisor introduces the relief teacher to the class (or classes) that day. This is a little difficult at secondary level but with a hard class it can be helpful because it validates the colleague in front of the class. The supervisor could say, 'Good morning, everyone. This is Ms L who will be teaching here while Mr M is away for a few days.' The supervisor may even stay for a while if the class is particularly difficult, and constructively team teach until the class is settled.

A brief word to relief teachers

If you are a relief teacher reading this you have probably been depending (in the short term) on relief teaching for your bread and butter. It is money hard earned. As one of my colleagues (Michelle) wrote in a letter: 'A new casual teacher on an upper primary class can be subject to a baptism of bulldust. Children delight in getting up to high jinks and the day can quickly degenerate into a "dump on the casual teacher" day. What the children perceive as an uplifting fix of fun the casual teacher may find a dose of insanity.'

There are a few basic things worth remembering:
- Get to school early enough. The last-minute haste of students arriving is not a helpful start to the day or session. If you can get into the room early enough it can help to check out the chalkboard, whiteboard, materials, room layout and so on. This is especially important at primary level. At secondary level be sure to take your own supply of chalk (replenish if from the office later), duster and so on. It's not worth the hassle of sending students to look for the basics.
- Make sure also that you have a key to the room, especially at secondary level.

- Avoid big discussions with students on who you are or why you are there. When I take demonstration classes the students often view me as a relief teacher. When lining up, several students call out loudly, 'Ay, you're not our normal teacher!' I think, 'Here we go again', as I usher them into class. I give a brief and positive good morning, with no extended discussions at the door. I say, 'My name is Mr Rogers. I'll be taking you for English today. Sit in your normal seat everyone.' There is no guarantee they will, and so later in the lesson I am prepared to relocate students. If you are with the class for a few weeks a class relocation seat plan my be helpful (p 28). It would be worth developing this with a colleague well known by the class.
- Check in advance (where possible) normative routines for the school or even for the year teacher (primary) for such procedures as lining up, sitting on the mat, toilet passes and so on.
- Have a separate tray to receive the returned notes for swimming, the excursion and so on. They'll easily get lost on the teacher's desk. I also find it helpful to have a tray for completed work to be marked. You may also find it helpful to direct students to do their work (if there for just one day) on paper rather than in their set workbooks ('I've lost my book Miss!'). Take in A4 paper with you, plus a box with all the writing implements including rulers (p 67) required. Photocopy key pages of any set textbooks (half a dozen for those without textbooks). In other words, be prepared.
- At upper primary and secondary level ask a trustworthy-looking student to do a seat-name-map when the student is settled (p 64).
- Know where the monitor list is at primary level.
- Have your own rules poster with you, just in case. Many of my colleagues who do relief teaching point out that this is a very helpful management device. Begin on a positive note to the day or session and introduce the rule reminder sheet. You could say, 'Good morning, everyone. My name is . . . [write it up]. I'll be taking this class today for English. Your regular teacher, Ms T, is not able to be here today. I'm aware that you have some class rules and routines to help us co-operate and learn well here.' Get that brief acknowledgment in early. However, you have checked the room, and there are no published rules anyway. It won't be helpful, especially with a difficult or reputation class, to ask, 'What rules do you have in this class?' Just acknowledge there *are some rules* and then add, 'Just to make life easier for us all I've brought the rules we'll be using today. You can see they're not much different from those you use with Ms T.' At lower primary it can help to have these rules in picture format. For example, the noise meter at lower and middle primary is a valuable novelty device that relief teachers can use (p 70). It is a simple way to remind students of what their regular teacher would expect for the hands-up rule and working noise during class time.
- From the outset manage behaviour decisively and positively. Give rule reminders early to the group (when calling out or engaged in private chatter) or to named individuals. This is not easy when the relief teacher does not yet know students by name. Eyeball the disruptive student. Ask the student's name. If a false name is given and class members laugh, avoid pressing the name, but just focus on the behaviour and the rule

specifically: 'We've got a class rule for asking questions. Use it, thanks.' If the student argues, refocus firmly and calmly. Avoid arguing or yelling or pushing the student into a power struggle. I had a student one day, on receipt of the invitation to give his name, reply, 'I've forgotten' in a sulky, clownish voice. I replied, as calmly as I could, 'Well, when you've remembered, let me know. In the meantime if you want to ask a question or make a point put your hand up without calling out or finger clicking. Thanks.' I then resumed the flow of the lesson.

- Set the work and behaviour standards early by not talking over student chatter or noise or accepting students who call out or butt in. Remind them of the fair rule. Acknowledge positive behaviours. This is not easy. Be prepared to do some brief follow-up. A notebook is helpful to record the names of students you believe need a follow-up chat or a class consequence. Avoid whole-class detentions (p 97).
- Be prepared to do playground duty (you're bound to score it).
- Avoid power struggles over teacher comparison: 'You're not as nice as our normal teacher!' Avoid the tempting reply to this sulky, attention-seeking five-year-old or 15-year-old: 'You mean the teacher who is in hospital with a nervous breakdown!' or 'I don't care whether you like me! I'm your teacher today, not Miss Snaggs. Get it!' It is enough to acknowledge and refocus to the essential: 'Maybe I'm not, but I'm your teacher for today and this is the work we're doing. How can I help you?'
- Avoid arguments over what their regular teacher allows them to do in class. This can be dealt with in part by knowing the routines (at least the essential routines) and by not arguing with the student (p 73/74).
- If the lesson material left for you is going to prove too taxing, in terms of communicating it to the students, it might be better to run with some tested and true lesson material (activities) of your own. It is not worth the stress of having to run a difficult lesson topic or activity that will put you behind the eight ball at the outset. Explain: 'The regular activity on . . . will be resumed when your teacher returns. Today we'll be doing . . .' It might even provide some curriculum relief for the class. Leave a explanatory note for the regular teacher.
- It won't hurt the class to have some busy work early in the day to get an understanding of classroom dynamics. I've often begun the day with some games—get-to-know-you games or communication games—but the point is to work within your comfort zone.
- Be aware (very aware) of the exit and time-out plan and how to use it. If anything, use it earlier in the cycle of disruptive behaviour rather than later, especially if you sense 'this is going to get very hairy if he keeps on behaving like this'.
- Have a notebook with you (p 85), especially on playground duty, to note students' names and behaviours that need following up.
- Follow up students who have left a mess, who were particularly rude or who were persistently disruptive (p 84/85). After all, you may be coming back to work with them again and it is worth setting good habits in train early.
- Finish the day as positively as possible (p 78).
- Leave the students' work marked (some teachers get a bit annoyed at having to mark other teachers' work).
- Make sure the room is tidy (even tidier than when you came).

- Leave relevant notes about any follow-up you have done or any 4W Forms (p 89).
- And make sure you return the cup!

When your class has given a relief teacher a hard time

If a relief teacher has been given a hard time by your class it is important to convey appropriate displeasure, even anger. Do not give a 15-minute (pacing) lecture, 'Who the hell do you think you are, eh?' Rather, give a firm, clear message about how their behaviour has affected both the relief teacher and you—a message conveying your strong feeling but geared to resolution not revenge.

You could say, 'I was really upset when I heard that this class, our class, had really given Ms S a rotten day yesterday. I was particularly upset that she had to hear comments like [here be specific], and put up with behaviour like [here give the worst, specific examples]. OK, maybe it isn't all of you [pause] but you all let it happen. I was upset for her [pause] and also that you would behave that way. I'm going to ask you to think about:
- how you can put this right
- what you can *reasonably* do now (after all Ms S had gone) and the next time you have a relief teacher.'

This exercise can be carried out as a class discussion or written activity. Most students suggest an apology and a list of things they can do to make the situation with the next relief teacher better: monitors assist with work distribution, a nominated student welcomes the relief teacher, students stay in normal seats, the class works by fair rules and so on. Of course, this approach works best when the regular grade teacher (or co-ordinator) has a positive working relationship with the class.

Thoughts of three relief teachers

> ### NOTES FROM A RELIEF TEACHER
>
> A student may continually nag you to change seats. An icy stare is the best rebuttal although you ache to scorch the recalcitrant with a terse, 'I said "no". Which part of no don't you understand?'
>
> Once the students are seated I state that these are our five rules for the day:
> 1 Hands up—no calling out.
> 2 Hands up—no coming out.
> 3 Speak and behave courteously and pleasantly at all times.
> 4 Today we do lessons Mrs Quirk's way.
> 5 Do your best work—neat writing, lines to be ruled with a ruler and no textas.
>
> Students calling out comments and questions or moving out of their seat at whim rarely works when a relief teacher is on the class. This freedom may be possible with the usual class teacher, but students may exploit this privilege with a relief teacher.
>
> Once the students are seated, remind them that it is required courtesy to let the teacher know if they want to leave the room. Despite this request students may leave the room without explanation during the day. When the relief teacher inquires about their absence they may give an abrupt reply, 'I needed a drink.' Remind the students privately, politely and quietly that they must put their hand up and ask next time.
>
> *Michelle*

REFLECTIONS ON ACTION PLANNING FOR RELIEF TEACHING

Rule posters were helpful in making expectations clear. In secondary music classes I put up some rules before pupils entered the room. My equipment rule—'Hands off unless you have permission'—was then clearly visible and could be pointed out straight away. This is essential when using Casio keyboards which, for practical reasons, needed to be set out on tables before the lessons. It also gave rise to some good-humoured interactions with the bright sparks who decided to interpret it as meaning they couldn't touch tables and chairs either!

Having name labels and making an effort to learn names was perhaps one of the *most* important things. I've only used labels with primary children. They seem to enjoy them and it makes it very easy to refer to everyone by name. I also found that *seeing* the names all the time helped learn them (I must be a visual learner too). After one afternoon in a reception class, I went back the following week and managed to remember several names without badges. I particularly remember the pleased 'glow' of a five-year-old girl when I asked her to collect the register and managed to use the right name.

In secondary classes, I made a point of calling a register and trying to put names and faces together. I always asked pupils to remind me of their names when they answered questions or when I was working with them, and apologised if I forgot their name. I'm sure this was appreciated and it certainly made me feel better. (Doesn't it feel awful standing at the front and wanting to address a pupil, but not knowing the correct name?)

It was helpful to know the rules and so on *already in place* in the schools. Teaching secondary music, I was particularly grateful to be able to remove one or two individuals on occasions (p 91) and knowing *reward* routines was good too. In one primary school the children could be given tokens in their group colour to store in a class treasure chest, which was counted up each week. It was a pleasure to give a token to one student, who I later heard very rarely got any. He had worked very well; I think this was as a result of my knowing him (and remembering his name) from a holiday club at church that he had attended. I found that children who had met me outside school like this (at primary level anyway) were very keen to be acknowledged *in* school.

Following up after lessons made an impression on both pupils and staff. It also helped me to focus on *individuals rather than classes* in difficult lessons at secondary level, and to remember that not all of the pupils were behaving badly. I wrote lots of notes to form tutors asking for help in chasing up missing books, homework and so on. Some of them did not appreciate this, but I did get good support from others which, in turn, made a difference to the behaviour of pupils in lessons (they know I know that the form teacher knows and so on).

Jo

Ros   Jo   Michelle

BEHAVIOUR MANAGEMENT ACTION PLAN FOR RELIEF TEACHING

Before going

Things to prepare and take:

• materials for lesson, including extras for early finishers
• box of equipment and materials to deal with 'I haven't got a pen' and so on
• rule posters/noise meter/help board
• 4W Forms
• notebook for jotting down names and so on to enable follow-up
• labels and ideas for games to help in learning names
• plan language/actions for discipline, including entry–exit procedures

At the school

• Check rules/routines/procedures with staff.
• Find out if time-out exists and how it operates (if not, ask to whom students may be sent if necessary).

In the classroom

• Explain cues, routines and rules to the class.
• Use discipline plan consistently.
• Note anything needing follow-up.

After the lesson

• Follow up if necessary and/or report back to school staff.
• Leave a note of work covered and so on for the normal teacher.

Ros

Chapter 9

SUPPORTING COLLEAGUES

The one important thing I have found over the years is the difference between taking one's work seriously and taking one's self seriously. The first is important, the second disastrous.
Margot Fonteyn

Expression means a personage.
Paul Tournier, The Meaning of Persons, *1957*

THE SUPPORT OF A COLLEAGUE

John entered the staffroom looking jaded and disoriented. Several staff were sitting down, talking animatedly. Teachers walked in, some acknowledging each other with a nod or smile. No one came up to him to say 'Hi' or 'How'd it go today then?' He felt like a stranger—out of place. Yet it was his first day of 'proper' teaching. He'd had a really difficult Year 9 maths class. The class at one stage had almost rioted. He thought, 'They didn't prepare me for this at uni—no way.' He sighed as he reflected on the miserable day. He was not sure where to sit down in the staffroom: 'Should I sit near that group—there's the head of department?' No one came up to him. He didn't feel one of them.

Still bemused, he saw a fellow teacher walk across. The teacher said, 'Hi, my name is David. I haven't seen you around before. First day here?'

'Yeah,' John sighed in return.

'Sounds as if it wasn't the best?'

'I couldn't believe how "off" they were! I just lost it with them. I tried being friendly, but they just didn't seem to care . . . ' John's voice trailed off in another sigh.

'You had Year 9? For maths?'

'How did you know?'

'I guessed. If it was 9L I can see why you'd feel out of it!'

The first-year teacher smiled, worn out but not defeated. He felt a little better. David said, 'There's a few of us working on a team approach with 9L. If you're interested, we're having a short lunch meeting tomorrow. Fancy a cuppa?'

The first-year teacher felt better. He'd found a colleague. The small act of acknowledgment and value as a fellow professional had cheered him. Support from a colleague makes a difference.

Acknowledge those areas in the school that already affirm colleague support. It can help to survey staff to ascertain what kinds of support exist already (Appendix 1) and what areas of need staff have in terms of general welfare as well as problem solving, action planning and structural support (Figure 9.1).

FIGURE 9.1

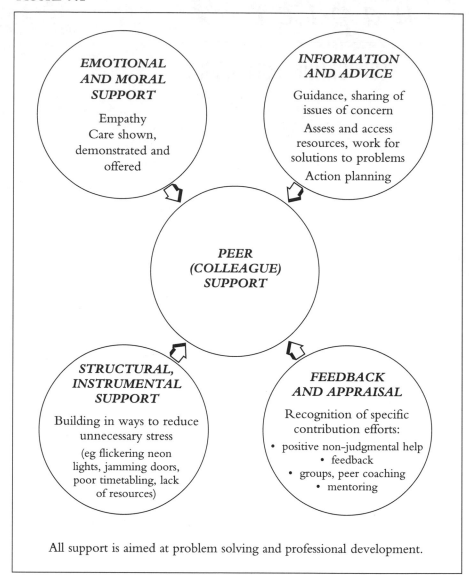

Where a school affirms the value of a supportive culture, staff know they are not battling on alone. Teaching can, strangely, be a lonely profession. When staff actively support one another it takes the pressure off feeling that one is 'totally responsible'. Colleague support also:

- reduces negative attitudes of inadequacy and/or self-esteem
- increases interpersonal problem solving and action planning
- increases coping skills, especially as colleagues work on common plans and access wider resources
- reduces the feelings of isolation.

Staff need to know that they are supported and can get support if they ask for it. Most of all staff need to be assured that they will be listened to with respect concerning their needs (Rogers, 1992).

Supporting colleagues who struggle with a hard class

It isn't easy to approach a colleague who you know, or strongly suspect, is having significant problems with behaviour management. In such situations teacher–pupil relationships may be strained and the delivery of curriculum and teaching approaches may be affecting class learning and behaviour. And yet if we know such a situation exists we cannot simply allow it to continue in the hope it will go away (it rarely does). Also, we cannot hold back on the pretext that approaching our colleagues about our concerns implies we think they are not good or effective teachers (which in some exceptional circumstances may well be true—in part at least).

So, how do we bite the bullet early in the cycle of negative behaviour of a teaching colleague so the issue doesn't become a perceived disciplinary performance review (which is always messy)? We can approach the problem in the following ways:

1 It can help to include in a school-wide survey on colleague support (Appendix 1) a focus question inviting school-wide colleague response on 'protocols of approach regarding teacher welfare and professional support'. In this way the issue is raised and everyone gets a chance to comment on this difficult issue. For example, preface the question with the following: 'From time to time teachers struggle with a class well beyond the BDS. Support is available at our school from the confidential chat through to mentoring and teaming approaches. The problem is that some teachers will not ask for support because they feel that other teachers may think they are weak or ineffective, or they may not be aware or believe they have a problem. In these cases it is important that senior colleagues approach their fellow teachers to ascertain what the problem is, and set up appropriate support. We don't want to hurt a colleague's self-esteem. We want to give support and assistance for the welfare of both teacher and student.'

    Question: If it was believed that a colleague had problems with their teaching and management, and there was evidence of non-coping:
    - How do you think that colleague should be approached?
    - What basic guidelines do we need to enable such a support process to occur?

    The responses normally cover issues such as:
    - maintain confidentiality (Don't call out to the colleague in the staffroom, 'Can I see you in my office Period 6 for an interview about 8C?')
    - provide a chance to share my side of the story
    - put the problems in perspective or in context
    - show me—don't just tell me
    - give me *time* to develop a plan with a supportive colleague.
2 Remember it's the first step of approaching a colleague that is the hardest. You could do the following:
    - Set up a meeting (pigeon hole note? private word?).
    - Tune in (briefly) to how colleagues might be thinking or feeling: 'You may be thinking . . . or feeling . . . about this meeting.' (They'll be anxious; they may even be feeling angry.)
    - Briefly share your concerns as you see them or know them from

reliable feedback (avoid the overuse of 'it seems' or 'I think'). The person running the meeting will need to be sure of the facts of their colleague's situation and 'performance' (the ongoing rowdy classes, and the complaints from parents and even other teachers and students).

- Be supportive and invitational in this feedback process and, above all, stay calm! This is the really hard point. Some colleagues can be infuriating with their avoidance behaviour, laziness, ineptitude, sulkiness and avoidance behaviours. It can help to plan questions beforehand, especially with colleagues who go silent, who procrastinate or who get angry quickly.

Be prepared, though, to listen. There may well be situations outside school causing stress and strain. Putting yourself in their situation will help. Acknowledge and affirm how such situations can well affect how one copes at school, but bring them back to the issues at hand—those at school. You could do the following:

- Invite feedback from the colleague as to their situation and performance.
- Use feedback questions, such as 'How do you see . . . ?', 'What's the problem?', 'How long has this [be specific] situation been going on?' and 'What do you believe you are specifically doing to address the issue?'
- Avoid interrogating.
- Seek agreement from your colleague that what you have identified is what is happening and that this is counterproductive and problematic, that it works against our school policy and that it needs addressing.

Finally get the agreement from the colleague on setting up a supportive due process to address the identified areas. Note them down, specifically, for an ongoing action plan.

3 Set up a supportive mentoring process. Have available several *mentors* from whom the colleague could choose to work with over a term *in the classroom:*

- to identify problem issues and teacher behaviours
- to look for areas where skill development needs to occur, based on supportive observation of the class
- to set goals and targets, and develop teaching and management plans to achieve this.

4 The mentor will observe some lessons (supportively) and then give feedback. From the observation and mentoring sessions:

- Give feedback that is descriptive, and supportive, such as 'Did you notice yourself say . . . ?', 'Were you aware of [for example, your characteristic body language]?' and 'I'd like to share what you said . . . Were you conscious of . . . ? Had you planned to say . . . ?'
- Acknowledge positive gains, and movement towards the goals and approximation of the skills.
- It can help peer mentoring to have the colleague observe some of the mentor's classes too.
- Work through the failure and BDS: 'What can you/we learn from this?'
- Review regularly and supportively.

Giving support is time-consuming and labour-intensive. It is also tiring. If you've developed a supportive, trusting, professional relationship, a lot can be gained. The earlier such support is offered, the more effective it will be.

Developing skills of confidence

Without in any way wanting to suggest that some teachers invite a hard time from students, there is no question that within the dynamics of teacher–class behaviours some teachers portray indecisive and non-assertive behaviours that can significantly affect student behaviour. This is no new phenomenon in schools either. Back in the 1950s I can recall a couple of teachers (both male) who had enormous problems managing the class in which I was a student.

One of these teachers would walk into class sighing. He had unusually baggy pants and his shirt was often hanging out. His face looked a cross between weariness, puzzlement, confusion and anxiety. He couldn't find the chalk and he'd ask us in a wimpish kind of voice: 'Where's the chalk, the chalk?' He'd often mutter, seemingly to himself. His voice wasn't clear—either in diction or range (and I'm not talking about loud). At times he seemed oblivious to us as he talked over or through the residual chatter. He was also very, very boring. He'd shuffle a lot and seemed unprepared—at least as we compared him with other teachers. Students are very practised at comparing and evaluating their teachers in terms of control, sense of humour, fairness (any favourites?), knowledge of their subject and provision of help, and also whether they embarrass you and follow up and so on. When this teacher got angry he really lost the plot. In fact some of the students worked out schemes to set him up and start him off. We gave him a hard time—from memory (1958). That practice hasn't changed either. Of course he didn't deserve it, but we didn't lose any sleep over it. That phenomenon is a hard *reality* of the teaching profession.

And that's the point. In the social reality of a school environment students will pick up on a teacher's dress, non-verbal behaviour, patterns of speech and *any* idiosyncrasies, especially confidence and assertion level. I'm not referring to aggression or loudness but the skill of assertion: the ability to convey one's needs and rights, the needs of the situation, or the needs of others, firmly, clearly and confidently. Assertive teachers can express anger appropriately and firmly. If they do lose the plot they are aware of it and seek to repair the break (if any) in the relationship quickly (BDN).

Teachers who are non-assertive and indecisive and lack confidence may well be in the wrong profession. However, if they wish to stay in teaching because they have a love of teaching and generally like working with children, they will need to develop skills of assertion and confidence, and the ability to convey enthusiasm, communicate anger, appropriately and so on.

If a teacher has been bullied by students (p 148), it may not be enough to deal with and even punish the bullies. We need to support our colleagues by enabling their skill development in the assertion of their rights to fair treatment. We do this with children who are frequently cast in the role of victims, so why not with adults? Part of our natural hesitancy in giving assistance may be that we are anxious not to convey that we believe they invited or deserved the treatment handed out by the students. Peer coaching is a very effective way to develop the skills that can empower them to do their job better.

Mentoring

A *mentoring* relationship can, over time, help the struggling colleagues; not in a superior–inferior way but as a trusted peer coach. We have set up elective mentoring where the teachers being helped select from several mentors on staff (confidentially) and then plan with their mentor a program of coaching.

The program involves classroom observation (mutual), feedback, identifying skill areas, learning and practising skills in a safe setting outside the classroom, and approximating the skills in the classroom setting. Modelling, rehearsal and feedback are essential elements of good coaching in any area—no less in teaching.

What is quite incredible in teaching is to believe that a good chat or access to a textbook is enough to see behaviour change in struggling teachers—it isn't. Of course, a process of change through peer mentoring requires trust, risk, time, willingness, effort and, most of all, colleague support, but the outcomes are worth it.

Confidence is both an attitude and a skill, each reinforcing the other. The key question to consider is what do confident people look and sound like? For example, if I stand in front of a class with shoulders heavily bowed and uncertain eye contact, shuffling my feet, smiling nervously and speaking with an overly hesitant voice, I communicate what the non-verbal behaviour is modelling. Non-verbal behaviour is a significant variable in one's confidence. It is all those behaviours apart from what we say that signal our confidence, optimism, enjoyment (or lack of it), our confusion and so on.

It can help to show a colleague (through video or gentle mirroring) what their characteristic non-verbal behaviours are like. This is a sensitive and difficult aspect of coaching, so it is essential to ask permission.

Remember a key aspect of behaviour change is feedback—supportive (descriptive) feedback. Both positive and the negative aspects of behaviour have to be addressed if successful change is going to occur. If colleagues are not aware of where they are ineffective, they may not be able to see a need for particular skills, or finetune the change process. For example, I've worked with colleagues whose up-front posture movement and stance actually 'contribute' to class entertainment. If colleagues are unaware that the way they stand, move and gesture is a factor in their management it will need to be gently pointed out. Even where they stand—or sit—can have an effect. I've worked with secondary teachers who sit down and do all their teaching from the 'sitting position'. This is less than helpful with more physically restless students whose behaviour and general motivation is enhanced by a teacher *standing up* and visually scanning the room, using a blend of visual teaching (on the chalkboard) and thoughtful class questioning and dialogue. In other words, *engage* the students! When I've gently mirrored what they do, some seem quite unaware ('Do I regularly do that?') and some can't see that it makes any difference. In that case the mentor will have to gently suggest alternative (better) practice and explain why it is 'better', and then work through the skills by modelling—rehearsal—feedback.

For example, there is little point in a colleague watching a mentor's class if there is not a framework for observational focus before the observation session(s) and a reflective and specific focus after the observation. If the colleague sees a 'successful' lesson (positive in tone, students on task, constructive learning exchange and a sense of calm), they may not know why the class was successful. *What* was it that the teacher (mentor) was doing that enabled 'success'?

Even when I've had very hard classes as a mentor and I've had to use time-out, I don't label my need for use of time-out as a failure. I invite my colleagues to see what we can learn about managing crisis situations (that is, 'What is an effective thing to say to an "off-the-wall-student"? How do you actually send for help? How do you 'calm' the other students?').

Key skill areas

It is necessary to identify the areas of concern. This is best done by mutual discussion and observation of the struggling teacher's classroom. There are several key skill areas (Rogers 1992).

Confidence comes with experience, yet experience needs to be useful and *informed*. Confidence also needs some success as well as the learning that comes from failure. Some *key skills in confidence* are the following:
- Stand relaxed but upright, with feet apart (not astride) and not wobbling or shuffling from one foot to the other.
- Scan the room with your eyes confidently when in the instructional phase of the lesson. Develop effective eye-scanning skills.
- Avoid a wobbly head. Focus and rest the gaze ahead during scanning.
- When speaking to individuals look in their eyes, with momentary relief now and then—it's not a stare.
- Speak clearly and use tactical pausing and a relaxed voice.
- Use an assertive voice tone and hand gestures (relaxed hand gestures, but not overly kinetic).
- Display an open face (not deadpan) and smile when appropriate.
- Have a flow and lift to the voice tone.
- Use open body language (not tensed up with arms folded tightly or legs crossed).

All these skills (macro and micro skills) need to be modelled by the mentor in 'safe' settings as well as classroom settings. Point out that each skill by itself may be small but it is the global impression that conveys confidence (Rogers 1995). I've worked with some colleagues who have a significant lack of social skill across the board—not just with children. Teaching is a profession that requires positive social skill. It can also help to conduct professional development in this area with all staff. It can help if the professional development session includes some powerful role modelling (by staff) to illustrate the range and kind of poor social skill demonstrated by some on the staff (without, of course, ever naming those staff members). If this is done with good humour, without directly pointing the finger, it can arouse awareness and need for social skill. When this is coupled with identification and modelling of positive social skill it can give a framework for ongoing staff development.

A (more) common belief is that group management skills are simply a natural gift. You either have it or you don't. Our evidence does not support this belief. Its most damaging feature is that teachers who have difficulty controlling classes tend to put this down to personal inadequacy rather than to a lack of particular skills which can be acquired through training or advice from colleagues.

The most talented, 'natural' teachers may need little training or advice because they learn so quickly from experience. At the other extreme, there are a few teachers for whom training and advice will not be properly effective because their personalities do not match the needs of the job. *It is clear, however, that the majority of teachers can become more effective classroom managers as a result of the right kinds of training, experience and support.* (Author's italics)

Teachers have tended to stay out of each others' classrooms and not to talk about their own discipline problems. Too often teachers do not seek help because it feels like an admission of incompetence, and they do not offer it because it feels like accusing a colleague of incompetence. As a result the tradition of classroom isolation persists in many schools.

The beliefs that either group management skills should not be necessary or that they cannot be learned seem to be traditional in part of the profession. Our evidence suggests that these beliefs contribute significantly towards teacher stress. This is further increased by the more widespread tradition of classroom isolation. We see these beliefs or traditions as barriers to good teaching. They should be removed as quickly as possible.
From Elton et al (1989), *The Elton Report*, p 69, recommendations 13–16

Personal, interactive skills relate to the following:
- A teacher relates to students in particular ways, for example, by the use of first names, pleasantness of tone and firmness when necessary, the use of greetings and so on.
- Many non-verbal skills are involved, such as use of eye contact, body language, tone of voice and clarity.
- Movement and proximity awareness are important. Some teachers are not aware of how to utilise a student's personal space, especially when the student may be in potential conflict with the teacher. For example, coming 'face-on' to a student may create unnecessary tension, especially when the teacher has closed fists pressing down and a facial glare.
- Some teachers are not aware, for example, of how they pace the front of the room, bob up and down, or wander during up-front instructional teaching time. Such behaviour easily invites overly physically restless students to unnecessarily visually track the teacher and not really listen.
- It is important to keep the flow of the lesson smooth and not jerky, as when the teacher is over-addressing discipline issues (Kounin 1970; Rogers 1990). One of the more important behaviours that signal confidence is the ability to regain composure quickly when one has made a mistake or briefly (we hope briefly) lost one's train of thought or even composure. It is the ability not to be easily flummoxed. It can be as basic

as the annoying tenth announcement on the intercom, something highly exciting happening outside, or the five students who came into the room (without knocking) asking if they can talk with the class about the coming school fete.

- Non-verbal behaviour such as *tactical* ignoring (not blind ignorance) should be used when necessary. I've worked with teachers who appear not to know what to ignore in a student's behaviour and what to attend to. They often attend to behaviours that can be ignored, and tactically ignore behaviours they should address.
- It can help enormously to develop a language of discipline (Rogers 1995). This involves having a number of key phrases and questions, where one doesn't have to directly think on the spot all the time.

It will be important to help mentors to address aspects of room and lesson organisation (bit by bit—don't overwhelm them) that are contributing to disorganised social and learning dynamics. *Organisational and management skills* relate to the following:

- Organisation may be lacking in basics such as how task directions are given, how equipment is utilised and monitored, how the teacher brings the students into class, and how the teacher settles the class and initiates attention. I've worked with teachers who 'lose' the class in the first five minutes because they do not seem to have any plan or focus.
- It is also important to address issues of student seating and grouping, how the lesson is normally paced and what rules/routines have been communicated to the students (and how).
- In some cases it may be necessary to re-establish the class (p 41), preferably at the end of a term ready for a more focused beginning the following term. A key role of the mentor/coach is to help sharpen that focus by identifying, with the teacher, the areas of concern; making a workable plan (bit by bit); identifying the skills and technique relevant to the area of concern; practising the skills in a 'safe' setting (with feedback); and approximating the skills in the natural setting of the classroom (with feedback). See Figure 9.2.

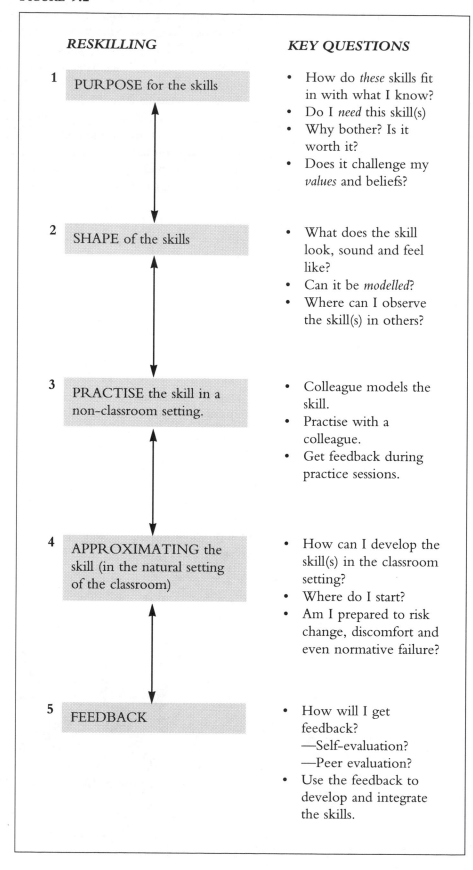

FIGURE 9.2

Teacher beliefs and attitudes

RESKILLING

1 PURPOSE for the skills

2 SHAPE of the skills

3 PRACTISE the skill in a non–classroom setting.

4 APPROXIMATING the skill (in the natural setting of the classroom)

5 FEEDBACK

KEY QUESTIONS

- How do *these* skills fit in with what I know?
- Do I *need* this skill(s)
- Why bother? Is it worth it?
- Does it challenge my *values* and beliefs?

- What does the skill look, sound and feel like?
- Can it be *modelled*?
- Where can I observe the skill(s) in others?

- Colleague models the skill.
- Practise with a colleague.
- Get feedback during practice sessions.

- How can I develop the skill(s) in the classroom setting?
- Where do I start?
- Am I prepared to risk change, discomfort and even normative failure?

- How will I get feedback?
  —Self-evaluation?
  —Peer evaluation?
- Use the feedback to develop and integrate the skills.

It may also be helpful to discuss teacher beliefs and attitudes that surface in the many one-to-one dialogues that occur in the mentor system. Beliefs such as '*No one* cares about me', 'I *never* get it right' and '*All* the kids have got it in for me' sap the psychological energy needed in teaching. Global language such as 'They *all* hate me' and 'It's *all* my fault' is part and parcel of some teachers' self-talk. It needs to be challenged and refocused.

As Seligman (1990) has pointed out, one's explanatory style has a significant effect on one's emotional state and hence behaviour. Perception is also affected by one's explanatory style—each reinforces the other. If a person's characteristic style of explanation of stressful events is defeatist and geared to failure ('It's me' and 'It will affect all I do'), the explanatory style quite likely *is* going to affect all that person does!

Seligman (and others) has pointed out that habits of thinking about and explaining events (especially stressful and bad events such as setbacks, difficult situations and failure) significantly affect the *events themselves*. 'Our thoughts are not merely reactions to events; they change what ensues . . . the very thought "Nothing I do matters" prevents us from acting' (ibid, p 7). According to Seligman we can learn the *skills* of disputing negative thinking and characteristic negative self-speech, and the skills of reframing situations to approach them less stressfully and more optimistically. This is more than positive thinking—it is the skill of 'non-negative thinking' (ibid, p 221).

I work with teachers who, in stressful situations, latch onto the most permanent and pervasive explanations for their stress, struggle or failure ('I'll never turn this around. It's all my fault'). This often discounts all the positive aspects of their teaching and their career and, instead of seeing their failure as an isolated situation, they globalise it as '*all* my fault' or '*all* their fault'.

Reality isn't that fixed! If we overfocus on a negative or stressful event or events at the expense of the many positive, good and healthy events, circumstances or relationships in our life and career, we allow the bad events an undue influence (p 13). An overly pessimistic *characteristic* explanatory style is a powerful factor in teacher stress (Bernard 1990) and performance.

When we look for *temporary* and *specific* causes we limit the pervasive effect of 8D or 9C, but if we explain that normative reality as redolent of all teaching and of all our performance as teachers it will increase general stress and probably lead to overall pessimism. That, in turn, will affect our esteem (especially self-esteem, the evaluation we place on ourselves relative to our circumstances, relationship and responsibilities).'Low self-esteem usually comes from an internal style for bad events: "I'm stupid", "I have no talent", "I'm insecure".' (Seligman 1990). Because internal self-speech is so often not reflected on (it is often a cognitive *habit*) people are not aware of the damaging effect of this 'psychological junk mail' (Rogers 1992).

It is possible to learn the skill of tuning into our thought and self-speech, catching ourselves saying the unhelpful, inaccurate or demanding thing: 'Children *must* respect their teachers.' The child had ignored the teacher's request in the playground. Instead of repeating this demand for respect semiconsciously the teacher can say, 'Hang on. It'd be better all around if the student did respond to my direction but he didn't. So I'm not going to get stressed about it. I'll note it down and follow it up later.' I've seen teachers race across playgrounds, fall over and have a psychological aneurism because of the *must win* belief.

I've learned the following:
- It is worth getting angry over issues that count, but not worth getting angry over issues I can't directly control.
- It is beneficial to give a safety margin to my anger—use assertive speech, control the voice tone beyond initial focus, attack the problem not the child, and keep the *expression* of anger brief.
- It is helpful to give cool-off time, and follow up later.
- One's negative self-talk needs to be challenged and disputed. For example, 'I *always* fail'—'Stop! You don't *always* fail. OK, you failed today when you . . . So we all fail now and then. Now, what can I learn from this or what can I do next time?'
- We can learn to choose more optimistic, realistic patterns of thought.

This is a skill, and it takes time. It's like tuning into a different radio station.
- When stressful events are occurring in our lives it can help to tune into what we're saying *about* those events, especially when the events involve people we're in conflict with. Self-talk is, after all, behaviour. It is our response or reaction to events. Realistic self-talk, rephrased self-talk, is a way of remapping reality. It is not the only way, but it is an important way.

One excellent text to assist in the coaching in this area is Kyriacou's *Essential Teaching Skills*, 1991. See also Grinder 1993; Robertson 1995; and Rogers 1992. In the area of teacher beliefs see Bernard 1990; and Rogers 1992.

Changing behaviour

Whether it is adults or students, behaviour change is never easy. It's not merely a matter of pointing out what's wrong as if from that stance one can simply access improved, new or different patterns of behaviour. People's behaviour is made up of emotions, attitudes and beliefs that have been shaped over time, and it often takes time to see consequent change in behaviour.

People's firmly held beliefs may make behavioural change quite difficult. I've worked with teachers, for example, who find *tactical* ignoring a very difficult skill because their belief (and attitude) is that students shouldn't ever answer back or have the last word. Consequently, a skill such as partial agreement or refocusing (as a feature of one's communication) is difficult to take up and utilise with conviction and—most importantly—within one's comfort zone.

If a student is leaning back in his chair, the teacher may give a reminder: 'Karl, four on the floor, thanks.' The teacher is about to engage the student by commenting on the work or task when the student sighs, 'I can still work like this.' (The voice tone is sulky and world weary—as if the student doesn't really care.) Some teachers will skilfully refocus this potential hassle by:

*   *tactically* ignoring the student's body language and tone of voice
*   partially agreeing: 'I'm sure you can still work like that'
*   refocusing: 'However, Karl, in our class it's four on the floor' (giving an extended four fingers downwards in a non-verbal signal and smiling)
*   adding: 'I'll come and see how your work is going in a few minutes' (thus giving him face-saving take-up time and a task-focused reminder).

Because the teacher's belief about such behaviour is flexible ('I don't like such rudeness, but it's his problem, and I won't let it stress me'), the teacher can genuinely tactically ignore some aspects of students' behaviour while keeping a behavioural focus through the use of language interactions and follow-up later if necessary.

Some teachers will overfocus on a student's secondary behaviour—the tone of voice, the sigh, the 'last word' and the marginal eye contact (Rogers 1995)—and the teacher and student are quickly in verbal conflict. The teacher's belief is that students *should* not be rude (they *should* be respectful). This pattern of belief drives the teacher's argumentative behaviour, making it hard (in some cases impossible) to keep the focus on what is primary in the transaction. Later, when teachers are rationalising these contretemps, they go back to the belief that shapes their attitude: 'Children *should* or *shouldn't* . . .' Because the belief is so demanding (p 141) and inflexible a skill such as partial agreement takes time to come to terms with. Just demanding that children *should* or *shouldn't* is not, in itself, going to change reality. Cognitive demands will also increase a person's distressful emotional state, whereas a more flexible belief can help moderate one's emotional state and, when coupled with thoughtful management skills, enable the person to be less stressed and more effective.

Changing behaviour is not merely changing belief *before* we change behaviour—it is working on both aspects of behaviour (cognition and action). Where teachers can see reasons for certain management and discipline behaviour (ways of relating and communicating p 72), it can help create the need that drives the risk of behaviour change. It is also helpful to explore skill development through beliefs and emotions. Learning new management and discipline skills is not the same as learning how to weld, knit or cook. Relational skills carry a lot of emotional and non-verbal cost beyond technical knowledge about what words to use in a given context.

When discussing the skills part of ongoing professional development, the following are important:
- The need for the skill has to be addressed, especially key language skills, organisational and management skills (for example, how to run a classroom meeting or how to run a more effective after-class chat). We need to address questions such as: Why do I need this skill? Who says it's important or even necessary? Why? and How will it help me? (Sometimes the latter question is merely utilitarian, but at other times it may be value added in that the questioner looks to the goal commensurate with particular skills.)
- It is important to address the willingness of colleagues. If one is not willing a mere half-hearted effort at new practices will create resentment when 'failure' is the early outcome.
- The 'shape' of skill needs to be seen, through comfortable role-play, hearing the language of discipline, having clear examples and even visiting a classroom to see skills and practices *in situ*.
- There needs to be a chance to practise the new (or improved or adapted) repertoire. Practice in a safe, small group environment can help. If practice can occur in settings where failure can be addressed quickly, then skill take-up is more effective. If one only has the hard class itself in which to practise, it can be self-defeating.
- Practice and failure are healthy partners. Failure can be a tough teacher, but when reflection and reappraisal are at work, progress can be seen and monitored.

I have worked with colleagues who give up on a program or a skill area because they won't hack the discomfort zone. Commensurate with skill development over time is the discomfort, the *natural* discomfort, of doing things (or saying things) differently: 'It doesn't feel like *me*', 'I prefer shouting!' and 'It was easier when I . . . '

In fact our stress level may well go up, initially, as we get used to different words, mannerisms or concepts. Even cognitive behaviour change— changing the way we think and the sorts of things we characteristically say to ourselves—can be stressful.

It will help the change process if we accept, and encourage others to accept, that such discomfort (even 'stress') is normative. The stress gets less uncomfortable as the new repertoire becomes 'personal', as it becomes 'one's own' and as we go from consciously ineffective to consciously effective (Rogers 1992). In time there will be days when the new skill becomes unconsciously effective. Change has occurred. See Figure 9.3.

FIG. 9.3

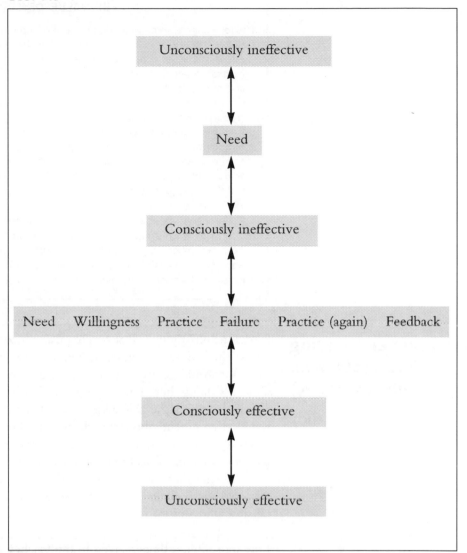

The following are also important in ongoing professional development:
- Feedback and colleague support are essential. Without feedback one may not be aware of how one's behaviour looks and sounds. Supportive non-judgmental feedback can assist in behaviour change in that a teacher can see how and where they are going with the skill(s). Of course, feedback needs to be elective, where possible, and mutual, and also non-judgmental and descriptive (not general). It should focus on a range of issues, and both the positive and negative aspects need consideration (that's the hard part). Most of all, feedback should be geared to mutual goals.
- There needs to be acknowledgment that change has actually occurred: 'Things are different now because . . . I am different now because . . .' (note the specific areas of change).
- The reflective habit must be kept going. There's no question that effective teachers are reflective teachers.

Teacher bullying (students who bully teachers)
Case study

It was the ghastly note that finally pushed her 'over the edge'. For many weeks she had been bottling up her anxiety and her frustration—she had hoped it would go away. It didn't. The Year 9 student was bullying her—almost 'stalking' her. The way he stared at her and eyeballed her, and the accidental look as he walked past her. Then it was the comments—the snide *sotto voce* comments about her clothes and her physical appearance. At other times it was the comments he made in class, out loud, that could garner the pathetic laughter of his little compliant coterie. Most of his comments were made when others were around so that the teacher (who was already clearly flustered and unfocused when this student was in the room) couldn't always be sure who said it.

Like most bullies he perceived in the teacher a weakness of character or personality that he could manipulate to his advantage. He had it in his head that this teacher was fair game and even deserved it—'it' being his ability to hurt others he felt were not OK. Such is the twisted logic of a bully.

He watched to see the increasing effect of his 'look', his words and his manipulation of the group. Like a gun firing bullets he could sabotage a lesson by sending out non-verbal cues to other members in the class who would also comment, disrupt a lesson or refuse to comply with a teacher request. He 'fired the gun' and sat back and watched his 'bullets' do the work. No doubt (like all gutless wonders) he felt the power of control—and that is what bullying is all about. The abuse of relational power (Rogers 1995) and the distorted and damaging control exercised by a person who believes he (or she) is more powerful, psychologically or physically, than the person selected to bully. The trouble was that she had let the insidious comments, the corridor laughter, the non-verbal signals that indicated physical acts, the group quiet as she walked past and then the laughter, and the whispered comments, go on and on.

But the note was the culmination. She had seen him pass it. It was disgusting. She had found the note (by accident?) on the floor after class. She'd recognised his writing though he hadn't signed it.

She took it to the co-ordinator after weeks of personal torment. Finally something was done. The student was confronted and suspended. By then the psychological damage had been done.

Individual and group bullying

Bullying is not accidental. It is not the occasional funny, ill-thought or stupid (if hurtful) comment about other people, their appearance, their voice, their mannerisms and so on. Bullying is the calculated and intentional desire to hurt someone else. It is the *repetitive* nature of bullying that makes it so insidious and damaging. The purposeful selective desire to psychologically control a situation so that another person is hurt.

The bully finds (and looks for) a target and then finds something about the victim they can exploit. Bullies will assess, through the responses of the victim, whether they have found a 'target'. If there is a non-assertive response to bullying comments or gestures (the victim looks pained, upset, confused, worried, anxious or fearful), the bullies know they have succeeded. Bullies may even believe they are justified in what they do because the victim is weak, stupid and different, and not like them. When a victim accepts the label given by the bully, the bullying behaviour will often continue.

I've seen male teachers put up with appalling comments about their clothes, their person, their perceived life preferences ('You're a poofter') and laugh it off nervously in the hope it will go away or try to get on the side of the students. All that happens is that the bully repeats their behaviour because it is confirmed by the victim's response. Bullying has to be confronted if it is going to stop. The earlier this is done the better it is for all.

Group bullying occurs when a significant number in the class emotionally support, or play 'patsy', to the bully's comment or behaviour. A bully who is allowed to become a key powerbroker in a group can make life 'hell' for a teacher:
• Rumours are often spread about the teacher.
• The class laughs when missiles are thrown.
• The class laughs at verbal put-downs of a teacher by a student, and will even laugh at verbal abuse.

Bullies, of course, select their target (a teacher who they believe will not fight back or assert the right to respect or follow it up with senior teacher support) or they make sure their bullying behaviour is indirect so that they can plead ignorance ('Me? Me? What did I do?'). Group bullying, because of diminished responsibility ('we're just mucking around'), makes such abusive practices easier for ringleaders.

The picture I have painted is bleak, but it happens in some schools. It happens for the following reasons:
• Some teachers tolerate it.
• Some teachers do not know what to do.

- Some teachers are not supported, because there is no direct 'evidence'. The worst comment I've heard from some teachers is, 'They [the bullied colleagues] bring it on themselves.'

No one deserves to be bullied. Teacher bullying, like any bullying, is wrong because it affects the fundamental rights of safety (physical and emotional safety) and fair treatment.

Dealing with the bullying of teachers
Preventative measures

It is crucial that the school has a clear policy aim within which any bullying behaviour is addressed. That aim is to create and sustain a safe environment within which students can learn and teachers can teach. The school policy will need to define:

- *Bullying.* The school policy needs to state exactly what bullying is, especially in its most common form—psychological harassment. Students will need to recognise that they are responsible for behaviours that are *calculated* to hurt (the snide comments, the ambiguous non-verbal behaviours, the missile throwing, the pretence to spit or vomit when a teacher walks past, the holding of the nose, the passive power struggles, the stirring-up of the other students, the spreading of rumours about the teacher and so on).
- *Due process.* This should outline clearly the sorts of unacceptable behaviours that constitute harassment (bullying), encourage the reporting and establishment of what is really happening, and give the assurance of a supportive hearing and the setting-up of procedures to confront the perpetrator(s). Due process should also outline the sorts of consequences that bullying will entail (right through, in serious cases, to suspension or expulsion). Many schools use the term *harassment* in their policies rather than bullying alone to highlight the more common psychological aspects of bullying behaviour. One of the hardest aspects of due process with bullies is confirming these behaviours as fact and, more importantly, establishing that the student's motivation is designed to calculatedly hurt rather than seeing it as 'having fun'.

One of the more effective ways to address this issue is to *empower the victim* (in a bullying situation) by confronting the bullying directly (often in a one-to-one setting with an adult colleague facilitating). The victim explains what it is the student is doing that is hurtful, how such behaviour is affecting the teaching and learning (and welfare) of the class, why it is unacceptable and that it must stop. This assertive clarification of how student behaviour is affecting teacher–class dynamics is a very powerful way to remove power from bullies by exposing the hidden reality of the behavioural dynamics. The facilitation of this process is crucial. A senior teacher will facilitate this process, keep records and evaluate outcomes (p 150). The earlier this process is established the more effective it will be. Where bullying is left unchecked for weeks or even months, the victim is so traumatised that they have lost any psychological will or courage to confront the perpetrators.

The school can do the following:
- Address bullying from a school-wide rights/responsibility focus. The clear policy perspective has to be the right to safety and fair treatment. Many

schools now have a published anti-harassment policy that puts bullying into proper perspective. Bullying is not the occasional stoush between a student and a teacher; it is not the task avoidance or task refusal that comes from BDS or the occasional power struggles that exist in classrooms; it is not the bad-day muttered swear word from students with low-frustration tolerance; nor is it students clowning around from time to time. It is the *repeated* harassment—the repeated unpleasantness to those who find it hard to address such behaviour or to defend themselves. Teachers who evidence low self-esteem particularly will find hurtful comments difficult because in not confronting them they 'accept' them. Their response through pained and anxious body language becomes, for bullies, the proof that their harassing power will work again. If bullies are not confronted early, decisively and assertively, they reconfirm their bullying status by a continuation of hurtful behaviour.

- Raise awareness. Schools often include the issue of harassment (bullying) as part of their human relations curriculum, raising key questions with students such as: What do we really mean by bullying? (This is to bring the more common definition of bullying into its more general expression of intimidation, threat and harassment rather than physical hurt.) Why do people bully? What do they get out of it (what are they trying to achieve)? Who has ever been bullied? How do people feel when they are bullied? How does it affect their life and their time at school? How do you think bullies feel? What can we do to stop bullying? What consequences are appropriate for bullying? How can we support victims of bullying?

- Hold a class meeting on bullying. It can be helpful for a senior teacher to run a classroom meeting on the topic with a class suspected of bullying a teacher. By raising the issue of bullying/harassment generally and inviting genuine responses, a teacher can point out that having fun like this (be specific about the harassing behaviours) is not a game; it is not funny for the person on the receiving end; teachers are not enemies; and it has to stop. It needs to be said, however, that students too need a due process to address poor teaching, unfair marking, and inconsistent and unfair management practices, especially students who have been unfairly targeted by some teachers. Before a class gets into some kind of perceived moral payback (class sabotage), it will help in such classes to pursue a class-meeting approach to give a voice to teacher and students alike to clarify and refocus their purpose for being together (p 30). Giving a lecture alone is not enough. A class meeting combined with individual student conferences can see a halt in any suspected harassment behaviour in the class. Bullying is a *learned* behaviour, a matter of choice. Of course, such behaviour choices are the results of twisted logic—by having an education program that explores the issue through values, beliefs and behaviour, the majority ethic is heard and upheld, and the bully's world view becomes the minority. Many schools run general classroom meetings on the issue of bullying as part of their human development program. I recall having a classroom meeting last year where I spoke to a high school class about how they had persistently mistreated their teacher. I said that no teacher deserved this and that their teacher had a life—she could have been their sister, aunt or mum. She was a person who had a right to be treated with basic respect and basic dignity. Because I had a good working relationship in the class, it had an effect. Of course, I allowed them their say as well.

- Report suspected bullying behaviour. An essential feature of due process is reporting suspected bullying behaviour. Bullying flourishes in a climate of secrecy or ambiguity of intent, as far as adults might perceive it. It is not a secret from a student's peers however—peer nomination and approval are needed for the bully's status. Research on schools that are high and low in bullying indicates that a key factor in low incidences of bullying is a climate of safe reporting and the belief that one will be taken seriously and that something will be done (see Smith & Thompson 1991, and Rogers 1995). I have worked with teachers who believe (sometimes mistakenly) that if they report their experiences they won't be taken seriously. Because of the apparent ambiguity of aspects of student-to-teacher bullying it may merely be taken as the teacher being unable to manage a class well, having poor classroom control, or being weak or inefficient. I have known some colleagues put up with continual harassment by an individual or a class for months until they break down in the staff room or the office ('I didn't want to cause any trouble!'). If we suspect harassment of any kind is occurring within a colleague's class (or even outside in the playground environment), we have a moral obligation to offer support and to assure the colleague that it can be addressed decisively and supportively. By allowing suspected (or known) harassment to continue we confirm its 'social legitimacy'.

Victim–perpetrator conference

One of the effective processes noted earlier is that of confronting the perpetrator or suspected perpetrator directly:

- Having discussed the issue of student harassment/bullying with a senior colleague, the victim identifies the perpetrator(s) or suspected perpetrator(s).
- The senior colleague sets up a formal meeting for each student named by the colleague.
- Prior to each meeting the colleague notes down specific issues needed to be addressed with each student. It can help (with teachers who lack confidence) to rehearse what to say to the student at the meetings and even write it down.

While this approach can be used by any teacher as a follow-up conference (without colleague support), there are occasions where a senior colleague can add moral authority to the conference process and indicate how serious the issue is being treated by the school administration. This approach is particularly suited to situations where students' behaviour is ambiguous or where they may argue that what they are doing is 'just having fun', that they weren't the only one (diminished responsibility), that they were bored in that class, that they don't like the subject or that they think the teacher is a lousy teacher.

It is also important when setting up an interview/conference to confront the perpetrators one at a time. If you put several harassers in a room, they will shift blame, laugh it off and back up each other. In short they have diminished responsibility *as a group*. This is why such behaviour can be difficult to address in a whole class of students.

The conference can be carried out as follows:

1 At the conference the senior colleague, as facilitator, sits facing the student and explains that they are very concerned about a number of behaviours in class such as . . . Here the facilitator describes, specifically, what they have seen the student do and say, or things the student has written that the teacher (the victim) has found offensive or hurtful.

2 The teacher then recounts how these behaviours have affected their teaching and ability to work with the group. This is the most emotional part of the conference as the teacher, looking their perpetrator in the eye, relives the emotions of the taunt, the back-handed comment, the hurtful laughter and the student's body language. It can help if the facilitator also makes some comment that relates to the behaviour in question. What is difficult in such a recounting is the avoiding of aggression so that the emotion is clearly heard without destroying the teacher–student relationship. By describing their feelings, the teacher is describing the *effect* of the offending behaviour. In some cases the student may not realise how hurtful their behaviour has been. By having to face (directly) the 'victim' it personalises the social transaction. If the teacher agrees (beforehand), the facilitator could mirror some of the tone and gestures to the student to emphasise the harassing nature of the behaviour. It is very important to list the non-verbal as well as verbal behaviour.

3 The teacher completes the recounting of events by looking at the student and asking them to stop these behaviours. The teacher can say, ' . . . [name the student] I want you to stop doing . . . [specify the key behaviours without going over the whole list again] so I can get on with the job of teaching here. I don't expect you to treat me in these ways. I don't dislike you but I cannot allow you to continue to affect learning in our classroom and my teaching.' It is important that these points are made briefly, clearly and firmly without aggression. Avoid a lecture!

4 The student is invited to respond to what the teacher has said. The teacher and the facilitator will listen to the explanations, but always keeping the focus on the fundamental *right* or rule, and also the school's policy on harassment. It can help to re-emphasise through a question how the student imagines the teacher feels when the harassing students do what they do. If the student argues, 'I'm not the only one who says stuff and laughs and all that!', the teacher replies, 'Maybe you're not. I'll be speaking to the other students who have been behaving in these ways, Lisa. For the moment I'm reminding you that we have a school *right* about safety and fair treatment and that we don't harass others here.' If the student continues to protest, re-emphasise the point: 'Maybe you didn't see it that way, Lisa, but when you frequently make gestures like . . . and say things like . . . then that is harassment. We cannot, ever, allow that at our school.'

5 If the student refuses to talk and sits there obdurate, it is enough to point out specifically that what the student has been doing or saying is against school policy and, more important, against fair rights, and that the student:

- has a right of reply
- is expected to change their behaviours (although we can hardly force an apology, it may be enough at this stage to let the student know that you know they know you know)
- will have to face the consequences of . . . if they choose not to change behaviour (this should be said without threat).

6 The student is then invited by the facilitator to make amends: 'What will you now do to assure [name the teacher] that she can teach in 8D without having to put up with these sorts of behaviours? What can you do (what do you need to do) to repair the damage to put things right?' Most students (not all) will apologise. An apology should be accepted, even if delivered sulkily. The facilitator can then ask what the student will actually do (not just *stop* doing) next time in class. This is written down.

7 The conference finishes with the facilitator saying: 'Lisa, we'll meet together in a week's time to see how things are going back in class.' The teacher(s) and student separate amicably.

The whole process can occur without the teacher being present. If the teacher is too upset or traumatised by the harassing student(s), then the senior colleague will go through these steps with each student one to one, although it is desirable that the affected teacher be actively present.

Suspected perpetrator Where the teacher suspects that a student is involved in some class harassment, even as a patsy, the teacher and facilitator can pursue the 'no blame' approach. I have adapted this from Pikas (1989). For example, there are students in the group who will engage in excluding behaviours that effectively lock the teacher out of the class group so that the teacher cannot effectively exercise their relational and role authority with the group. The following steps may take place:

1 Outline what has been happening: 'Carly, I'd like to talk with you for a moment about what's been going on in our class.' Of course, the facilitator can pursue these issues on behalf of the class teacher, for example 'Ms G has been hearing a lot of comments such as . . . [be specific].' Let the student know that you are interviewing a number of students in class, not just one student.

2 Invite comment/feedback: 'What do you know about this, Carly?' Again the process is both a genuine attempt to elicit information as well as letting the student know you are 'on her case' (even if you have no direct proof).

3 It can be helpful to outline how the teacher feels when this behaviour is going on, or ask the students how they think their teacher might feel. I pursued this approach once with several students who merely thought they were having fun (with a non-assertive teacher). Several of the students had some involuntary tears (tears I hadn't intended). They all apologised to him (as a small group), though they asked if I'd be present at the formal apology (I suspect to convince me they were serious about making amends).

4 Note down the student's observations and feedback, even if the student

suggests that the teacher's behaviour may be contributing to some of the harassing behaviours. Some teachers will benefit by being aware of behaviours that easily elicit student hassling in a group (in terms of group dynamics). The way some teachers dress, speak (those idiosyncratic behaviours that look unusual or funny), adopt mannerisms and so on can affect student perception and give easy rise to comments, gestures and laughter. This is not to excuse the way some students behave, just to explain reality. If the behaviour in question is particularly offensive it will be important to add: 'No one deserves this kind of behaviour because they look or sound different, or act in a way you don't like. If you've got a legitimate complaint about a teacher, you know we'll speak with that teacher or even have a class meeting.' Finish by saying: 'OK, I've made a note of your observations/comments. I think we've talked long enough.'

5 Reaffirm the school's behaviour code/rights (briefly) and set up the second meeting to review with this student 'how things are going back in 8D'.

With a suspected perpetrator the teacher/facilitator does not apportion blame. They describe and acknowledge what is happening, asks questions and leaves the student with the responsibility to, in effect, let the grapevine do the rest.

If the bullying behaviour is serious, the school will need to pursue full due process via the anti-harassment policy. This will involve parent conference, suspension and even (in some cases) exclusion.

The key to dealing with bullying is to make sure the climate and ethos make it difficult for such behaviours to get a foothold. This will occur if the school has a climate of safe disclosure and a supportive colleague ethos where people look out for one another, and if early intervention into bullying incidents is the norm. The school needs to:
- have clear whole-school policy guidelines and due process
- develop teacher skills of assertion, confidence and behaviour management with those teachers who are non-assertive and lack important behaviour management skills.

As Smith and Thompson (1991) note, 'If you get it out in the open, you have a better chance of dealing with it.'

Occupational stress

Stress is fundamentally the pressure or demand placed on one's coping abilities. Teaching is a *naturally* stressful occupation: a multi-demand profession where we are constantly on the go. Those stressful demands range from the hard class, and the challenging and even disordered students to the constant marking, evaluation and support of students' learning.

Stress is exacerbated, though, by the structural irritants that frustrate one's daily role:
- Neon lights may flicker and be noisy (I've taught in semi-darkness rather than have a loud buzz).
- There is not enough student furniture (seats/tables). This is largely a secondary school issue. It's frustrating to have to send a student to another

class for seats, let alone the hassle of students doing a last-chair grab.

- Some furniture is badly scarred and damaged. Of course, students do the damage, but the longer it is left (or if not followed up at the time of damage), the more it validates the overall jaded aesthetics of scarred walls, doors that jam, windows that are hard to open, blinds that don't work and so on.
- Some heaters don't work and some are even dangerous.

These basic structural concerns are essential and, most of all, remediable. Schools cannot afford to ignore basic occupational welfare and safety.

Other issues of concern that contribute to daily stress are:
- last minute room changes (now and then it is fair enough but . . .)
- not having a key to the classroom (especially for relief/supply teachers)
- poor and even inadequate timetabling
- lack of support and back-up with behaviourally disordered and challenging students, poor time-out planning and provision, and inadequate follow-through and tracking of BD students.

Most of all it is the belief that one is not taken seriously—is not valued. It is essential to emotional welfare and safety that senior staff listen to the concerns and needs of teaching staff. They can then work on ways to eliminate *unnecessary* stressors that are putting pressure on an already stressful role.

It is worth surveying staff each year (at least) on issues of concern regarding 'structural stressors' (Rogers 1992 p 29).

Chapter 10

CONCLUSION

But haven't we been painting a word picture of an ideal state? True. Is our picture any the worse drawn, then, because we can't show how it can be realised in fact? . . . Does practice ever square with theory? Is it not in the nature of things that, whatever people think, practice should come less close to truth than theory?

Do you agree or not? I agree.

Plato, The Republic, *Book 5, p 472*

This has not been an easy book to write. Constantly reflecting on the hard classes I have had and those I've worked in with my colleagues has brought back some tough memories. I can recall the stress and strain and the hurt that some students inflict on their teachers. Trying to put that reality into perspective, and then into print, has concerned me a little—mainly that the reader might gain the impression that this is the way *schools* are. It isn't. Most students and most classes in most schools do get on well with their teachers (BDN). The hard-class syndrome is, however, a reality and it has been my attempt to address the issue *as a teacher*.

You will need to read other books if you want to explore socioeconomic or sociocultural perspectives on the behaviourally disordered preconditions affecting schools. That is not my brief. I'm concerned here with how my colleagues and I can realistically cope with hard classes and how we can make a difference. Genuine colleague support can help put the hard-class syndrome back into some perspective.

Teaching is a job that can 'eat up' your life: marking, following up students, planning units of work, fiddling around on the computer to get the right 'feel' to that worksheet, making individual education plans, more marking, meetings, more meetings, taking work home, designing posters, organising the room, more meetings and so on.

When we get a hard class it seems to dominate our perceptive; we don't look forward to the day or that timetable slot. We may easily allow that class an unrealistic place in the overall scheme of things. What I mean is that we may be overfocusing on the behaviour of the class (or key individuals) and not seeing all the other positive aspects of the group or even all the other positive aspects of our teaching: our contribution to the school, the times when things have gone well and so on.

It's like looking at a white square that has a black dot in the centre. If we are not careful, thoughtful and aware, we may see only the black dot—the worse elements of our stressful situation at the expense of the many (often much more) positive aspects of our teaching, the students and even of life itself!

That is not to deny the reality of the black dot—the presence of stress, produced by difficult and demanding students, hard classes, pressure and tiredness, and emotional pain. Denial is, itself, unhealthy—even dangerous. See the black dot for what it is—it is there, it is demanding, I have to cope with it and come to terms with it, and I can. What I won't do is let it dominate my teaching and my life, so it is the only thing I see in the square (p 141).

Earlier this year my daughters and I swam with wild dolphins in Port Phillip Bay (actually they were very civil). We left the pier at Sorrento in a largish boat equipped with wetsuits, snorkels and flippers. There were about 20 intrepid dolphin lovers on board.

As the boat cruised the bay, our professional dolphin tour leader explained that when a pod of dolphins was sighted we were to get into the water quickly and hang on to a line running back off the stern. We would be gently towed through the water and, if we looked below us, we would see the dolphins swimming around underneath us. He also explained that we were there to entertain them, not vice versa. 'What do you mean?' I asked. 'Well, sing to them; they like singing.' I thought of my singing voice and reflected it would be more likely that I'd scare them away. But no, I was assured dolphins like happy noise—not loud, but happy singing.

Eventually, as the boat trudged the bay, a pod of dolphins was sighted. Several dolphins were leaping, with flashing tails, in the late afternoon sun. We even saw a baby dolphin. 'In the water, quickly!'—our guide beckoned us to drop off the back of the boat and swim off onto the two trailing lines held up by buoys at the stern. My oldest daughter and I swam out. There were about ten of us along the two lines stretching from the stern. Our leader said, 'They're coming—now underneath you!' and then said in a loud whisper 'Sing, sing!'

No one sang; their heads were under water trying to glimpse what we'd all come for. I thought I'd better kick off a song or two. I could only think of the Italian song 'O Sole Mio!' And it's hard to sing under water through a snorkel! Worse, I couldn't remember the Italian words, so I sang (in pitch, with bubbles, in the cold, green water of the bay): 'Oh sole mio, I've come to see you. I only paid 50 dollars but I know it's worth it . . . Oh sole mio;

I'm here to see you . . . ' You understand that I sang the refrain with a snorkel and Italian accent (no offence) and so I raved on. And they came! Two huge grey and scarred bodies, bottle-nosed with that unique smile dolphins have, slid underneath me as I held a line. My daughter called out (under water), 'They're coming, Dad!' The two bodies rolled over each other, smoothly and gracefully as they swam a metre underneath us. It was fantastic. Everything else, for a few moments, paled into the background. One of the dolphins looked up at me; its eye seemed to lock on me. I smiled and said, 'Hi.' I don't know if the dolphin registered that I was an underwater teacher also scarred by life's vicissitudes! But as I looked at my fellow creature it helped to put back a bit of perspective in my life. It was a great day, a great experience. One day—God willing—we'll do it again.

It is important to have a significant life outside teaching to find healthy and creative ways to put our stressed lives back into perspective. It may be a film, a long walk in the bush, music, a night with friends, hobbies, a book, a relaxing drink and chat or even a swim with dolphins in the bay.

It is important to keep the perspective so that we don't overfocus on the black dot in an otherwise white square. The black dot can, if we're not careful, overly affect (even infect) the positive areas of our life. Try to do the following:

- Avoid letting a bad day (or bad days) affect all the other areas of your life, especially your life outside school. Our partners, children and friends don't deserve the entrails of 8D replayed unthinkingly in our home or elsewhere.
- Avoid the easy blaming of yourself when things are going wrong and you can't seem to get the class focused or on track. If you have honestly tried and have sought (and utilised) colleague support, you have done your best. Failure, bad days and genuine mistakes (that result from tiredness and work overload) usually have only a temporary effect (Seligman 1990) and if we're aware of that reality we can learn from it. As Noel Coward succinctly put it, 'The secret of success is the ability to survive failure.'

- Avoid the unthinking rating of self, 'I'm not as good a teacher as so and so.' All teachers struggle at times with their teaching and management role, but not all teachers admit it. I was conducting a workshop some years ago on colleague support and a teacher of 30 years' experience surprised his peers by sharing (publicly) that the Year 7 he was teaching had really caused him to reassess his teaching and management. This admission, in itself, was a source of encouragement to his younger colleagues—'*you* too'.

I hope this book will be useful as a way of reclaiming a sense of perspective with your hard(er) class(es). Most of all, I trust it will assist in the process of giving and receiving colleague support—the support that can make all the difference.

Appendixes

Appendix 1: Colleague Support—Staff Questionnaire

The issues listed here provide a basic framework for developing a staff questionnaire.

Preface

This questionnaire forms a part of the process of reviewing colleague support in our school. Of course, the issue of colleague support can range from the relaxed conversations with a colleague through to how we plan together and communicate across the school. It can cover issues such as structural support (where we support one another through time-out provisions for difficult and demanding students) as well as issues such as peer mentoring and staff appraisal.

We are concerned to ascertain how you perceive colleague support at our school—both its strengths and limitations. We also wish to define and improve areas in which colleagues have concerns or perceive a lack of support.

This questionnaire is, of course, confidential and all results will be communicated to staff at the earliest convenience. The feedback and opinions from the questionnaire will form a basis for review and action planning in future team-facility meetings and whole-staff planning sessions.

If you feel comfortable it would help the utility of the findings to note:
- the grade or subject area you teach
- the years of teaching experience you have had.

The questionnaire

1   What does colleague support mean for you—as a teacher?

2   In what areas do you believe colleague support is operating effectively at school (tick boxes):

☐   planning of lessons; units of work; use of resources

☐   problem solving on issues of concern (such as discipline and classroom control)

☐   back-up support in difficult management situations (such as time-out)

☐   follow-up with difficult students (such as holding a conference and conflict resolution)

☐   colleague mentoring and appraisal.

	Very confident	Confident	Only if I really push it	Not confident
3 a How supportive are your team leader, head of department and administration (deputy/principal)?	☐	☐	☐	☐
b What sort of support do you receive from these colleagues?	☐	☐	☐	☐
c What sort of support do you look for from these colleagues?	☐	☐	☐	☐
d In what ways, if any, could such support be improved?	☐	☐	☐	☐
e How confident are you of receiving support from your team leader/year level co-ordinator, deputy or principal?	☐	☐	☐	☐

4   a   Looking back over your teaching career, what kind(s) of colleague support have you most appreciated?

_____

_____

Why? _____

b   Are there any models of colleague support—ways of working together—you have found helpful in other schools that you believe we could benefit from and apply here? Please summarise.

_____

_____

_____

5 a If you believed you needed support in the area of behaviour management or lesson planning from a team leader or senior administrator, how would you normally initiate such support?

_____

_____

b If administration had to support a colleague whom they believed needed support and assistance in areas such as behaviour-management, classroom control and teaching strategies, how should such an approach be made?

_____

_____

c What should the senior colleague consider when approaching and offering support? (This is assuming that the colleagues have not initiated any support themselves or that they do not see they have any concerns or problems, or if they do they are not acknowledging those problems.

_____

_____

6 In what areas here in our school do you believe colleague support is difficult to obtain and why?

_____

_____

7 Do you have any concerns about colleague support (or lack of it) in this school? If so, please note those concerns (it would help if you could also note why).

_____

_____

8 In what ways are your skills, abilities and contributions acknowledged here at school? Please note the ways.

_____

_____

9 To whom do you normally turn for professional guidance and advice that you can count on?

_____

10 Do you have any suggestions, beyond those you have already noted, about how we can develop a more supportive culture here in our school?

_____

_____

Appendix 2: The 4W Form

Student's name [ ] Class [ ]

Teacher's name [ ]

Subject [ ] Date [ ]

Student comments

What I did against our class or school rules

_____
_____
_____

What rules (or rights) I broke or infringed

_____
_____
_____

What is my explanation?

_____
_____
_____

What I think I should do to fix things up or work things out

_____
_____
_____

Teacher's comments only   Date

_____
_____
_____

Resolution required (please tick)

☐   Total exits from this class

☐   I will work through the conflict

☐   I will arrange a time with my year level co-ordinator (home class issues)

☐   I will arrange a time with the subject co-ordinator (subject issues)

☐   I need the intervention of the year level supervisor to work with me and the student

Return to year level co-ordinator

Adapted from a SA pro-forma statement. Note that this form may have various names, for example Personal Response Sheet, Student Response Sheet or Behaviour Response Form.

Appendix 3: Stop/Start behaviour plan

MY GOALS	
STOP DOING	**START DOING**
1 _____	1 _____
_____	_____
_____	_____
2 _____	2 _____
_____	_____
_____	_____
3 _____	3 _____
_____	_____
_____	_____

- Is your plan achievable?
- OK, how will you do it? Discuss this with your teacher.
- How will you handle 'bad days'?
- What support will you need from your teacher?

Appendix 4: The 3W Sheet

OUR CLASS!

Please record your answers on a separate sheet. Thanks!

So:

1   What's working well in our class?
      What things (activities and the way we run things) work well in our class and why?

2   What's not working well and why?
      Anything upsetting you? Why? (If personal, put it in writing.)

3   What are some things we can change? How?

      Let's discuss together.
      Let's make a plan for action:
      a   Things we can start soon
      b   Things that will take a bit longer
      c   How we'll do it.

Appendix 5: No put down zone

NO PUT DOWN

Bibliography

Amis, K 1996, *You Can't Do Both*, Flamingo, London.

Barnes, R 1994, *School Discipline: Some Guidelines for Students*, University of East Anglia, Norwich.

Barrish, H H, Saunders, M & Wolf, M M 1969, 'Good behaviour game: Effects of individual contingencies for group consequences on disruptive behaviour in the classroom', *Journal of Applied Behaviour Analysis*, vol 2, pp 119–24.

Bernard, M 1990, *Taking the Stress out of Teaching*, Collins-Dove, Melbourne.

Biggs, J & Telfer, R 1981, *The Process of Learning*, Prentice-Hall, Melbourne.

Brown, D, Reschly, D & Sabers, D 1974, 'Using group contingencies with punishment and positive reinforcement to modify aggressive behaviours in a 'Head Start' classroom!', *Psychological Record*, vol 24, pp 291–496.

Caffyn, R E 1989, 'Attitudes of British secondary school teachers and pupils to rewards and punishments', *Educational Research*, vol 13, no 3, Nov, pp 210–20.

Conway, R 1974, *The Land of the Long Weekend*, Sun Books, Melbourne.

Dalton, J 1985, *Adventures in Thinking: Creative Thinking and Co-operative Talk in Small Groups*, Nelson, Melbourne.

De Bono, E 1985, *Conflicts: A Better Way to Resolve Them*, Penguin Books, Harmondsworth, UK.

Dempster, M & Raff, D 1992, *Class Discussions: A Powerful Classroom Strategy*, Hawker Brownlow Education, Cheltenham, Vic.

Department of Education and the Arts, Tasmania 1990, *Positive Discipline: Improving Behaviour in Your Classroom*, Hobart.

Doyle, W 1986, 'Classroom organisation and management', in *Handbook of Research on Teaching*, ed M C Whitrock, Macmillan, New York.

Dreikurs, R, Grunwald, B & Pepper, F 1982, *Maintaining Sanity in the Classroom*, Harper and Row, New York.

Elton, et al 1989, *The Elton Report: Discipline in Schools*, Report of the Committee of Inquiry, Her Majesty's Stationery Office, London.

Embling, J 1987, 'Dark and bloody side to young life today', the *Age*, 2 June, p 22.

Glasser, W 1991, *The Quality School: Managing Students Without Coercion*, Harper and Row, New York.

Goffman, E 1972, *The Presentation of Self in Everyday Life*, Penguin, Harmondsworth, UK.

Gossen, D 1992, *Restitution*, New View Publications, North Carolina.

Green, C & Chee, K 1995, *Understanding ADD*, Doubleday, Sydney.

Grinder, M 1993, *Your Personal Guide to Classroom Management*, ENVOY, M Grinder & Assoc, 16303 NE 259th St, Battle Ground, WA 98604, USA.

Harris, S J 1973, *Winners and Losers*, Argus Communications, Niles, Illinios.

Hill, S & Hill, T 1990, *The Collaborative Classroom*, Eleanor Curtin Publishing, South Yarra, Vic.

Johnson, D W & Johnson B T 1989, *Leading the Co-operative School*, Interaction Books Co, Minnesota.

Johnson, L 1992, *My Posse Don't Do Homework*, St Martins Press, New York.

Jones, P & Tucker, P (eds) 1990, *Mixed Ability Teaching: Classroom Experiences in English, ESL, Mathematics and Science*, St Clair Press, Rozelle, NSW.

Kounin, J 1970, *Discipline and Group Management in the Classroom*, Holt, Rinehart and Winston, New York.

Kyriacou, C 1986, *Effective Teaching in Schools*, Basil Blackwell, Oxford.

Kyriacou, C 1991, *Essential Teaching Skills*, Basil Blackwell, Oxford.

Lewis, C S 1943, *The Abolition of Man*, Collins/Fount, Glasgow.

McCarthy, P, Freeman, L, Rothwell, C & Arnheim, B 1983, 'Is there life after 8D? Group reinforcement at the postprimary level', *Interview*, no 11, Ministry of Education, Victoria.

McGrath, H & Francey, S 1993, *Friendly Kids, Friendly Classrooms*, Longman, Melbourne.

McInerney, D & McInerney, V 1994, *Educational Psychology: Constructing Learning*, Prentice-Hall, Sydney.

McNeil, C 1994, *AD/HD Classroom Kit—An Inclusive Approach to Behaviour Management Instruction Manual*, Centre for Applied Psychology, PO Box 61586, PA 19406.

Morgan, D P & Jenson, W R 1988, *Teaching Behaviourally Disordered Students: Preferred Practices*, Merrill Publishing Co, Toronto.

Nelsen, J 1987, *Positive Discipline*, Ballantyne Books, New York.

Olweus, D 1978, *Aggression in School: Bullies and Whipping Boys*, Hemisphere, Washington, DC.

Pearce, H (in press), *Groupwork in the Classroom*, Cambridge,

Pikas, A 1989, 'A pure concept of mobbing gives the best results for treatment', *School Psychology International*, 10, pp 95–104.

Robertson, J 1995, *Effective Classroom Control: Understanding Teacher–Pupil Relationships*, 3rd edn, Hodder & Stoughton, London.

Rogers, B 1989, *Decisive Discipline: Every Move You Make, Every Step You Take,* Video-learning package, Geelong Conference Centre, PO Box 280, Geelong, Vic. 3220.

Rogers, B 1990, *You Know the Fair Rule,* ACER, Camberwell, Vic.

Rogers, B 1992, *Supporting Teachers in the Workplace: Teacher Stress and Collegial Support,* Jacaranda Press, Milton, Qld.

Rogers, B 1994, *Behaviour Recovery: A Whole-School Programme for Mainstream Schools,* ACER, Camberwell, Vic.

Rogers, B 1995, *Behaviour Management: A Whole-School Approach,* Scholastic, Gosford, NSW.

Russell, D W, Altmaier, E & Van Velzen, D 1987, 'Job related stress: Social support and burnout among classroom teachers', *Journal of Applied Psychology,* vol 72, no 2, May, pp 269–74.

Rutter, M, Maughan, B, Mortimer, P & Ouston, J 1979, *Fifteen Thousand Hours: Secondary Schools and Their Effects on Children,* Open Books, London.

Seligman, M 1990, *Learned Optimism,* Random House, Sydney.

Serfontein, G 1990, *The Hidden Handicap: How to Help Children Who Suffer from Dyslexia, Hyperactivity and Learning Difficulties,* Simon & Schuster, Sydney.

Smith, P K & Thompson, P 1991, *Practical Approaches to Bullying,* David Fulton, London.

Tobias, S 1989, 'Tracked to Fail', *Psychology Today,* Sept, pp 54–60.

Tournier, P 1957, *The Meaning of Persons,* SCM Press, London.

Wood, E & Knight, J 1994, 'I feel sorry for supply teachers: An ethnographic study', in *Introduction to Research Methods,* ed R C Burns, Longman, Melbourne.

Wragg, J 1989, *Talk Sense to Yourself: A Program for Children and Adolescents,* ACER, Camberwell, Vic.